D0848489

Uncharted

Lines

Uncharted Lines

POEMS FROM
THE JOURNAL OF THE
AMERICAN MEDICAL ASSOCIATION

Edited by Charlene Breedlove
Preface by John Stone, MD

Boaz Publishing Company
Albany, California

Distributed by
Publishers Group West

Address all inquires to:

Boaz Publishing
PO Box 6582
Albany, California 94706
510 525 9459

First Edition

Edited by Charlene Breedlove
Preface by John Stone, MD
Designed by Elizabeth Vahlsing

Library of Contress Cataloging-in-Publication data:

Uncharted Lines : Poems From the Journal of the American Medical
Association / edited by Charlene Breedlove ; Preface by John Stone.
—1st ed.
       p.   cm.
ISBN 0-9651879-4-2
   1. Medicine—Poetry. 2. American poetry—20th century.
3. Physicians' writings, American.   I. Breedlove, Charlene.
II. Journal of the American Medical Association.
PS595.M43U53 1998
811'.5080356--dc21   98-29375
                                                      CIP

Printed in the United States of America

The Poets

BEGINNINGS: A PREFACE

by John Stone, MD

*I*n New Jersey to give a talk, I've arranged to make a brief visit to the city of Rutherford, to a house at 9 Ridge Road. This address, for decades, was both office and home for William Carlos Williams, the physician-writer whose name is well-known to readers of this anthology. Dr. Williams practiced medicine in Rutherford, where he delivered 3,000 babies and tended his ethnic working-class practice. It was here, too, that Williams wrote the tough-minded muscular poems that changed the face of American poetry (and won for him, posthumously, the Pulitzer Prize). Today's visit is one I should have made while the elder Williams was still alive. It's a kind of pilgrimage for me, then—and for some medical students who've joined me.

The number "9" appears in two places at the entrance of the tan Victorian clapboard; there can be no mistaking that this is the place. I knock and Dr. William Eric Williams swings the door open. The older of WCW's sons, William Eric still lives and practices pediatrics at this address. He invites us in and we take our seats in the waiting room. WEW begins by telling us some anecdotes about his famous father, then starts the tour.

William Eric is a wiry man whose facial features and general build are clearly indebted to his father's genes. Even his voice is wiry, plain-spoken and certain of itself, the reassuring voice a parent would like to have in a pediatrician.

On the walls are reminders that WCW was deeply involved in— and moved by—the art of his time—works by Marsden Hartley, Vasily Kandinsky, Charles Sheeler, a couple of originals by Charles Demuth. In fact, WCW was an artist himself: a self-portrait is partic- ularly well-known. In contrast, on the walls of the examining rooms are cartoon drawings of animals designed to hold the attention of WEW's little patients. "Gotta keep 'em smiling," he says.

He shows us a small room where William Carlos did a lot of his typing. I feel privileged to be here despite William Eric's warning that "it's just a regular office." "But," I demur, "there must still be some of your father's atoms around the place." "I expect so," he replies, grinning: "He did tend to sneeze quite vigorously!"

On the second floor is "the north room," made famous by one of my favorite poems by Williams, "Danse Russe." The poet depicts himself in that room, dancing "naked, grotesquely" before the mirror and singing softly, "I am lonely, lonely. / I was born to be lonely, / I am best so!" The poem ends this way:

> "Who shall say I am not
> the happy genius of my household?"

The attic is cluttered and dusty, rendered most memorable because of some material that WCW tacked on the walls: newspaper articles, postcards, memorabilia that had some special significance for him 50 or more years ago. Especially poignant is a long graph of the plummeting Dow Jones average during the Great Depression.

William Eric is joined now by his wife as the tour moves to the living room. They show us the leather-bound volumes of his work that WCW gave to his wife, Flossie. And lots of photographs: WCW as baby, as intern, as dapper young physician. On the wall is an early photo of Ezra Pound, instantly recognizable because of the shock of unruly hair.

I thank the Williams for the privileged tour and we shake hands. Before we leave, I take one last photograph of William Eric Williams, hands in his pockets, in the entrance way to 9 Ridge Road.

After the flash, he asks me, "Did you get the '9' in the picture?" I did.

William Carlos Williams is literary godfather and mentor par excellence to many of today's writers, most especially poets. His work (not only poems, but short stories, plays, an autobiography, and novels) and his personal example no doubt strike a responsive chord among many of the writers represented in this anthology. Like the contemporary painters whose work he admired, Dr. Williams found poetry in the objects, the "things," of daily life: the red wheelbarrow, the plums in the icebox, the woman giving birth with a mighty effort ("Not a man among us / can have equaled / that").

The poets represented in this anthology have interests just as diverse. And the subjects that have engaged their eyes and ears are provocative and moving: Alzheimer's and music, transplants and obesity, Chekhov and Schubert and Manet, healing, joy, death, and love. It goes without saying that it is good to see the names of some of my friends appearing as authors within these pages, the more so because I had nothing whatsoever to do with their selection.

Within this preface, I want to remind us all of the heritage that is ours because we are writers—or readers. I want also to include here two etymologies that are worth keeping in mind. The first is the Greek word *poiein*, which means "to make." The medical word hematopoiesis, "the making of blood," derives from that source. So, happily for our purposes, does the word poet, which means, therefore, "a maker." All the writing that follows, then, is done by poets, in the best etymologic sense of that word.

The other etymology I have in mind is that of the word epiphany (from the Greek, *epiphaneia*, "appearance" or "manifestation"). An epiphany, of course, is "a moment of sudden intuitive understanding, a flash of insight." The writers in this anthology, many of them involved in some way in health care, experience epiphanies all the time: To hear another person's medical history is to walk straight into a poem or a short story, an experience that easily qualifies as an epiphany. Listening to such a history can be not only the beginning of diagnosis, but the beginning of art. Every patient is his or her own art and it's up to the doctor, the nurse, the listener, the poet, the writer— to find it. The writers included herein have found—and recorded— the epiphanies of their lives meticulously and in fine style. We are indebted to them. They write to make sense of the world and to capture the moment. And thereby they are themselves renewed and sustained. And so are their readers.

Cesare Pavese, the Italian poet and novelist, wrote, "The only joy in the world is to begin." To begin may not be the only joy in this world, but it is a mighty one. And since we are poised here quite near this book's beginning, let us do just that. I congratulate the poets, salute the editor, and declare this joyful project officially begun.

Introduction

by Charlene Breedlove

Poetry related to medicine, along with poetry in America generally, has burgeoned over the past decade, becoming a recognizable genre in its own right. But, then, what experience cannot be found in some way connected with our biological self, our life and death? As health and medicine encompass ever more of our public and private concerns, the rising response from those whose lives brush against illness or the threat of illness seems a vibrant sign.

The sudden onset of a disease, the impersonal setting of high-tech scans and procedures, an uncertain diagnosis or treatment outcome—even witnessing such events in the lives of others—all carry home the scent of our mortality and profound vulnerability to the unknown. To answer the thousand questions such events stir, we endow them with personal meaning, giving visibility and voice to our passage. Hence the casting forth of lines of poetry that seek to chart one's sense of crisis and loss in relation to a lifetime. Whether as patient, doctor, friend, care giver, or observer, we often struggle to come to terms with the odd tensions and paradoxes generated by the medicalization of human encounters. The wonder in this may be simply that in the face of deep uncertainties, poetry remains the language of choice, the only language that gives solace to the soul and revives the imagination.

Poetry's appeal lies in its ability to offer both writer and reader a moment's transport. However painful the circumstances, when creating the language of poetry, the poet leaves the strict literalness of words; customary roles fall away, and the boundaries of relationships—in particular, the writer's relationship to conventional and scientific speech—dissolve. Words in a poem are free to form novel patterns and rhythms, to honor elusive feelings and unfinished thoughts, to interact with one another and in so doing to liberate the writer from the burden of purely rational expectations and thinking. Poetry thus serves to restore a sense of wholeness, of being in touch with the many parts of one's generative self.

The healing powers of poetry have been recognized since the Greeks paid homage to Apollo, whose heavenly lyre could reweave human rendings of body, soul, and spirit. In our time, we individually summon the powers of healing through the magic that still resides in the sounds of words spoken in a certain way in certain combinations. The language of poetry today and the poems in this collection being for the most part free verse, the reader will have to attune his or her ear to each poem to catch the resonances between sound, rhythm, and intentionality.

Many of the poems speak a direct, almost prosaic language; some are more refined in their use of poetic techniques, some are simple narrative poems, a number are slyly or cleverly or playfully humorous. I chose these from among the hundreds published in the Journal for qualities that have as much to do with the kinds of experiences being conveyed—that is, what the poem defines as an experience and who the experiencer becomes—as the language itself. While an editor always seeks an appropriate balance between what is said and how it is said, in poetry these become inextricable. If a poem seemed to me unpolished, but I felt it brought forth something authentic and worth attending to, I included it. I also selected for freshness and variety, to display the many ways people have of perceiving, conceiving, and coming to terms with what unsettles us. My hope is that in reading these poems others will feel an increased range of empathic possibilities and insights open to them and that they will carry this "imagination" with them as they interact with the rest of the world and with themselves, whether in sickness or in health.

Uncharted Lines

POEMS FROM
THE JOURNAL OF THE
AMERICAN MEDICAL ASSOCIATION

Morning Prayer

There is more to
it than the
clomp and stomp, the
constant bipedal
hoofbeat of the
gear boys and
their Cordura packs, more
even than the
aesthetics of the
stunning contrasts and
dizzying humus, there's
the disappearance of
bone, the weeping of
skin and muscle, the
here and *this*, the
constant chew, grind, and
gulp of evolution, the
metronome of your
breath and the forest, the
diffused light of early morning,
the first slow,
full inhalation of
dawn.

Jay S. Auslander

Geometry

I am fragile
like glass, torn
by the hard
geometries of
living, the sawtooth
boulders of the
Bio-Bio, the isosceles
corners of each
flip of the
calendar, the angles of
broken twigs and
shards of fragmented
hopes. It's math
that does this: the
right angles and
divisions, crusty π and
arid algorithms. Perhaps
the tinkerers see
the end: How what
pulses but portends
the geometry of the skeleton
that no longer bends.

Jay S. Auslander

The Med Tech Explains the Differential

> The normal individual has a large marrow
> reserve . . . which can be released
> in response to sudden need.
>
> *Introduction to Hematology*

After work,
exhausted,
eye muscles
strained to buttons
behind my lids,
I dream them: cells
forming and falling
in eggshell white
protein skies:

lymphocytes
with china-blue rims,
their centers dark
as if a heavy-handed child
had colored them in,

neutrophils,
imperfect spheres
with azurophilic
flecks of dust,
their nuclei
a series of fists
joined by inky filaments.
The fragile, ashen monocytes
with ragged vacuolated edges,
tissue paper flowers,
wandering ghosts;

sometimes
an exotic Turk,
dark angry prowler
in an indigo mask,

or plasma cells,
sensuous half-mooned
harbingers of pain,
Cassandras of the marrow's
passion turned obsession.

Then come the blasts,
those overblown balloons
with pale uncertain
centers,
released
before the end
of the parade.

I wake
with vertigo
as if I too
were floating
in the microscope's
white glare,
falling
from a source
I cannot name.

Jackie Bartley

Poet Dying of Alzheimer's

—Hotel Dieu
New Orleans, 1991

Diagnosis

I do not fear death
by water, by fire, by ice.
I fear such courage.

I fear death by unweaving,
the husks of images,
the stone tongue.

Darkness laps up my light,
my pool of knowing,
the mirror of "I am."

Cocooned in void,
I will lie nameless,
doubt made flesh.

I am the word unspoken,
the coiled question
in the orchard of innocence.

Requiem

We celebrate the end
of your heart's song.
This is the blessing
we have prayed for you.
This we have learned from you—
a crystal in the dark.

Now! You are going out,
guttering weary on a spent wick,
your death comes as a lover
dancing you around a new sun,
whispering the semantics of silence,
gifting you with shadows.

Judith Boudreaux

A Bellevue Story

Marvin, you came to us out of the Bowery,
limbs, skull, and ribs fractured.
Unconscious, in shock, more dead than alive,
a mangled piece of dirty, stinking humanity.
Hit and run on the street,
they said you were bumming a drink.

We drilled burr holes in your fractured skull,
drained your bloody subdurals.
You awakened!
Your rib cage shattered, we tubed, then trached you.
You breathed for us.
Alive but not well, your saga began.

You survived the sepsis of your Foley, and the DTs.
Strapped down, you raged.
We knew you were healing when old habits returned.
"How 'bout a smoke, Doc?"
I lit up a cigarette.
Puffed through your trach, it was your only pleasure.

In the ebb time, after midnight, wired in traction,
your popliteal pseudoaneurysm burst.
Red invaded the white of your plaster pants.
We descended on you, buzzing our Stryker saws,
like drones serving a queen.
But it was too late to save your leg.

I lost track of you in Rehab, Marvin.
It was your sixth month in Bellevue.
Walking on your prosthesis didn't come easy,
the nonunion of your tib-fib fracture, the AK amputation.
But you survived it all, and left us after a year.
Rumor had it you were wintering at the Miami VA.

I saw you last in Admitting, that following spring.
Back in town from Camp LaGuardia,
you were on the streets once more.
Your prosthesis broken, you crawled the gutters.
They carried you in on a stretcher.
I called the social workers.

We were happy to see you again,
in need of a cleansing, but still surviving.
I found you a bed, disinfected you.
We repaired your broken prosthesis
and a little of your broken life.
Marvin, you had plenty of visitors that day.

Richard Bronson, MD

Engines of Healing

They'll toboggan the silver bore
of a hypodermic needle.
They'll thread their way
into my cells,
find the missing linkages,
rewind my DNA
like a videocassette,
making me vigorous,
hearty and hale;
artistically rearrange
a deficient pancreas,
an unproductive alveolus;
nibble plaque from artery walls,
gobble the odd neoplasm
like mechanical macrophages.

When it's time to self-destruct,
will one decide to stay,
stake out a homestead
in unexplored territory—
perhaps an intestinal villus
or my corpus callosum—
and self-replicate?

Will I become the known universe
to a nanomechanical race?
Will future generations speculate
whether I'm expanding or steady-state?

Shirley A. Cody

Last Concert

Lipatti at Besançon, France, 16 September 1950

Between the applause and the houselights' demise
among nervous coughs and pale sunshine in Besançon
Amid a hush now so intense we hear our own hearts beating,
We wait to hear Dinu Lipatti play his last concert.
We know he is ill with a grave and mysterious illness,
We hear it is lupus erythematosus. We fear he may not play.
We know his doctors have advised him against this performance
Because he is weak and febrile, but he has been given
The new American cortisone and perhaps he can perform.
He will play a program of Bach, Mozart, Schubert and Chopin.
We know he never plays without intense preparation.
Ah, now he is at the piano, there is a silken trial arpeggio,
An agonizing silence, and then the architectural Bach. . . .

But the Schubert, the *Shubert!*

Incredible that one artist is dead and the other sick unto death,
Incredible that we hear the voice of Schubert across time
In the imprecise precision of an artistry that weighs and measures
With unerring taste, that says to us this is what the master wrote
And did not write upon these pages and this is what I a dying man
Sick from a young lupus offer you as a testament of his genius, perhaps
Of mine. You may hear this music again at other times, other
Places, but it will not be the same, it will not be his, mine, ours,
It will not hold the enchantment of these reaching moments
It will not breathe of attar of roses or of wolfsbane.

Manuel Cooper, MD

Passage

Charon, here is your freight for Styx the black river
No coin under his tongue to buy his bleak crossing,
Our age's offering struck from the weaving loin
Anomalous spirit formed in the ichor of spent cities
Knowing all to know of hate before the chance of love
Love, he has asked, *What is love? Someone to watch
Over me?* Caught now in some desperate enterprise
He has fled from his deed and met the spinning slug
That robbed his brain.

Ferryman, when first we dreamed, you were a blazing dot,
Fierce brightness, moving slowly upon Lethe,
Your face too veiled to see, your boat too dark to view.
When you met Achilles, did you call him murderer?

We have, failing, done for our man the best we could:
The brain faltered before the heart, and we helpless
Have ripped the trace from the pen, the animal magic gone,
And have brought him to this marble bier, waiting for you.
Who now dares place a penny in his quiet mouth?

Should you ask him *Whence?* and *Whither?* if you care,
You old man in dirty rags, as we have last dreamed you,
With something dark and strange dripping from your silent oar,
He may not answer, he may not know, he may have only you
To be all things to him now, his boatman and his judge.

Manuel Cooper, MD

Where's Roosevelt?

Where's Roosevelt? she calls
across the parking lot.
As wind cuts the thin sheet,
she sees his podium
is gone. The medics pinch
a facemask to her nose
and squeeze the ambu bag.
The cars are gone, his stars
and stripes are nowhere
to be seen. *Where's Roosevelt?*
They roll her past the place
he spoke in 'forty-four.
Weeds. Glass. Cracks. Curb. Where's
the dressed-for-Sunday crowd?
Where's the squash? And rows
of beans to beat the Jap?
Where's the widow
who carries to his chair a box
of V for Victory vegetables?
Glass. Bottles. Cans. *Where's
Roosevelt?* She twists and spits
the mask, and struggles
with her strap. *Shush, babushka!
Shush!* They slide her stretcher in
and clamp the locks. *Ah yes!
Now. Now.* She tastes his smoky breath
and feels in this dark place
the root of Roosevelt's thin legs
against her groin, and welcomes him.

Jack Coulehan, MD

My Uganda

for Sister Concepta Najjemba

On an African afternoon
in Pittsburgh
sister scans the hills
for burning weeds
for whatever she sees
is Uganda.
She sips lemonade
on the steps of her porch,
watches the roofs
for menacing birds
and suffers sleeplessness
for sleep is Uganda.
Sister's pale blue habit
is a vista so distant
that barefooted runners
as tough as fugitives
carry tales
across its landscape.
Surrounded by the spoor
of Africa, she sways
on her porch, telling tales
of midnight raids
and dead cattle,
of her father
shackled to a chair
where they shock him
in the balls,
of her brother
necklaced to a tire
doused with gasoline
and set afire.
When sister speaks
about the tragic fever
that carries her country
out of its senses, her body is
Uganda
frightened
delirious
insensate
and holy.
While all the other

sisters sleep, Uganda sits
on the edge of her bed,
jerking and swaying.
She runs her hands
along its thighs
and whispers mai mai
softer
than the vibrating fan.
Sister's fingers
ripple through the dark
and sister prays. Her prayer
is medicine, her prayer
is sweet,
sweet medicine.

Jack Coulehan, MD

Adelaide

I imagine the chilly room
where the Death Committee sits
at five o'clock—an icy slope,
with Adelaide

across a wide crevass.
The seven hundred grammer can't
take enough by lung or gut
to make it on her own. It looks

as if . . . The docs, her nurse,
an aide who turns her, the worker
with his words about the mother,
the risk manager—

We climb together in a world
where taut compassion is a rope
around our waists
connecting us. But Adelaide

lies in a land encased in ice
like a fist without an arm.
Her chromosomes are added wrong.
Number one, the mother's gone

to a disconnected number
in the Bronx. And number two,
she's bled again, her brain
has plugged the fluid in.

Number three, there may be pain
in this small fist: she's grimacing.
I imagine tossing a rope
across the crevass. No one

catches it and then it snaps
into darkness. Our hands are frozen
from the trek, our limbs are sick
as we turn back.

Jack Coulehan, MD

Lachrymae Rerun

Fried flounder on cardboard plates, slaw,
drafts of dark beer. Pain has followed us here
to the fish place in Riverhead. I'm fed up
with clammers' shot backs, bad kidneys,
and their wives' arthritis. I'm fed up
with cancer wearing suspenders and dousing
its flagrant heart in wine. The tables here
are crammed with pain. The coolers
are stacked with eel, like black,
pickled sausage. Go ahead, though, keep talking
about your cancer's home—the church
you grew up in, its baroque Italian priest
and pinched nuns that scuttled across your youth
like bugs. You're not buying it—not an ounce
of original sin, not a word of Augustine,
nor anything that carries you down
from joy. That's what you *say*. Even the walls
of this joint are sweating blood, but you've
converted to a new belief—the cosmic dance.
Go ahead, keep talking, I'm not thinking now
about the sweating bodies of the dead
in Africa, nor that woman with the bomb
beneath her t-shirt in Sri Lanka, nor the kid
gunned down in Brooklyn, nor the arrogance
of righteous violence. I'm trying to imagine
the original blessing. Go ahead, tell me
the wizened eel of history is somebody's fault—
Jesus' or the popes'—and if left to ourselves
we'd surely dance. And be compassionate,
tender. Go ahead, finish your beer
and let's kick up our heels. It's Saturday night
in any case—and I'm tired, too, of tears.

Jack Coulehan, MD

Chekhov's Doctors

3. Ragin

Wherever I look, the world
is dense with lack. Ignorant towns.
Small tasks. The withering
absence of progressive thought.

The world is jaggedly obscene
with injustice—
the patients in the wards
are prisoners, the prisoners

in the jail are sick. The front
you wear—a toss of luck.
The sickening stench of things
creeps into my appointed rounds

of pacing, beer, and books.
Routine doesn't give me the solace
it once did, and loneliness
drives me to lunatics

for talk. The passion I spent
in youth (little enough) is gone,
but the craziness of passion
has come back to knock me—

into the locked ward,
where Gromov abuses me
with his barbed wit. I have yet
to experience suffering,

but want to. To the watchman
who carries the key,
the difference between us
is illusory.

Jack Coulehan, MD

Chekhov's Doctors

10. Gaev

The end of the century
has come upon us
without a sign of release
or the beginning of justice.
We're selling the orchard
to pay our debts
and reminiscing about
love's excitements,
life's mistakes. I suspect
a century ago the hearts
of the people sitting here
were just as generous,
intense, and cruel as ours.

A miniature flower
thrives in the moisture
and dust of a broken
pavement——this is the gist
of the matter. We want
so strongly to believe
the flower will spread
everywhere. How quickly
it dies! If the disease
had a cure, we would not need
so many remedies.

Jack Coulehan, MD

Chekhov's Doctors

11. Dorn

Not to take the play seriously
would be frivolous, but to interpret
the story. . . what's the point?

I tell them clearly the damp air
is miserable here—my role, after
all, is reason—but the truth is,

no matter what I say, all of us
will suffer before the play ends.
And when a seagull appears

in the second act, it's simply
a dead bird, but Chekhov
is tricky—he wants to convince you

it means something. Stick to the facts,
I say, stand aside until they need you—
there's nothing medicine can do

to solve the riddle of love's suffering
or any suffering. Toward the end, though,
they'll call me to watch the damage.

You want to say tragedy, don't you?
Take it from a man who's worked in blood,
this is comedy instead—the way we are

before that final shot explodes.
Of course, in this production
I conceal the truth about the shot—

a despondent lover drills his brain
with lead, but I come back
to the boy's mother and say, *It's just*

a burst bottle. I've found deception
is a card worth playing.
Beneath my breath I whisper the truth,

Get her out of here. Her son is dead.
And remember the dead gull
in the second act? In the last scene

it's stuffed. There you have it—
our good friend Chekhov is playing
at symbol. It isn't very helpful.

Jack Coulehan, MD

Chekhov Answers His Critics

No, I haven't forgotten
progress' story—
the students bellowed it
across Russia
when I was young.
In their march
to establish justice,
they left me behind—
I suffered from a
lack of passion
and a pair of good eyes.

My sainted old father—
I haven't forgotten him
either. He puts on
peasants' clothes
and devotes his estate
to the poor. The purpose
of poetry, he says,
is the turning of conscience.
Still, the meanness
that exists in us exists.

Nobody wants to like
the ordinary—
yet the peasants
are brutish, the anarchists
cruel, the "superfluous men"
are supremely superfluous,
and any one of us,
if given power, could turn
as brittle as the czar.

The heart is a peasant
who warms himself
around the fire
of unspeakable treasure,
a chained convict
awaiting the day
of his imagined release,
a buffoon in the marketplace.

There's humor in this,
and pathos—
so night after night
I scribble my infamous tales
and peddle them. Let others
invent our redemption.

Jack Coulehan, MD

Lovesickness: A Medieval Text

As real as melancholy, baldness, headache,
or scalp lice. As real as Christ's love for his bride
the Church. As real as an imbalance of bile
in the brain's ventricles, tumbling the lover
ever forward with sad sighs and hidden thoughts.
As real as the surge of moist heat that collects
in the second ventricle and thus creates
in the first, a cold, dry atmosphere—stunned sense.
As real as a parched mouth, an edematous tongue,
a bitterness in the throat, as though the patient
had eaten unripe plums. As real as rapture,
but as pale in complexion as spent humor.

Cures include travel, which diminishes languor
and permits the beloved's image to lessen
in potency. The deep induction of sleep
by medicinal herbs, which wipe clean the slate.
Wine, conversation, and the reading of books,
which serve as cathartics, purging the patient's
obsessions. Litigation, or bringing a suit,
may also be helpful, by putting an edge
on the mind's collapse. In the most serious
cases, all these remedies are likely to fail—
in such cases, prescribe sexual relations,
following which a cure will usually occur.

Jack Coulehan, MD

To a Bosnian Poet

The poet is the one who starts over again.
Izet Sarajlic*

Do you remember how we dreamt of mountain peaks
Covered with snow
And hoped our nation, too, would grow up one day,
In spite of the convulsions
You thought were caused by childhood fever
Bound to pass without consequences, whatsoever.

Would you ever have thought
The tower built of our dreams
Could be doomed by the Balkan fairy
Said to destroy by night
What mortals built by day;
The orthodox descendants of Prince Marko plowing the railroads,
As if the tracks were Turkish roads;
The brethren of Pontifex
Blowing up the bridge in Mostar.

Would you have thought, trivial as it may sound,
A bespectacled medicus from Croatia
Might read your poems on American prairie land
Convinced the carnage would not have happened
Were more poetry of yours read in those cursed mountains.

Is there any hope I could still reach you,
In that morbid lupanar of folly?
To learn what happened with the Pushkin books
That belonged to your White Russian neighbor;
Whether the dew is still on the fruit tree at dawn
And to ask you, if you know:

How much poetry will we need to start over again.

Ivan Damjanov, MD

Izet Sarajlic, a poet born in 1930 in Bosnia and
Herzegovina, lived most of his life in Sarajevo.

Sonnerie de Saint Genevieve du Mont

after Martin Marais

It could have been in the mountains
at the compulsive turn when winter gives
way to spring. In the afternoon sun
the village children, as surely as their parents,
understand that soon a warm wind will push
the ice away.

But it happened in a hospital room.
One doctor, a nurse, a woman about to give birth.
The music she had known for some time
plays itself through her body.
The bass line imitating church bells:
at once dull and urgent.

In her confusion she perhaps stands on a mountain,
where she watches a constellation of seed capsules.
The stubbornness of roots. Persistence of green.

The violin and harpsichord cling
to the melody, as the gamba marks time.
Each line chooses a part of her.
If you looked closely you could discern.

It was said that Marais (violist
to the King) played like an angel.
Angels, for whom there is no choice of existence.
He fathered fourteen, many of whom took up gamba.
Such a sawing, one can't imagine.

Now she focuses on the viol.
The figures in the room shift places; as if
in slow motion or an intricate court dance,
where their feet glide imperceptibly over the floor.

She hears her doctor's voice, at once gentle and
commanding, over the gamba line.
Her muscles respond, as a string of eighth
notes shudder through her body.

She clings insistently to this music,
as if it will transport her to the
mountainside, where already quill weed
and wild cucumber have erupted in a finale.
She is ready now to confess to anything.

Carol V. Davis

Visiting the Lightning Struck

I imagine Moses, his tablets burned by God.
But this is nature's wrath: a man
whose skin is charred, with ragged ports
where bolts raged, piercing heart and lung.

Unlike holy, dead-aimed strokes,
this summer lightning flash cracked
down and back, fused his corneas like opaque glass and
burst his eardrums as if they were balloons.

Did fear come with, before, or after?
And did he see, or simply feel, bones smoke,
eyelids melt? When heart stopped,
did he gasp and wait until the tick resumed?

Or did the lungs freeze first, then
the other organs fail? How will he think
of picnics after this, how love August's
hazy light—where bees drone air thick

as saturated gauze—until the cumulus
swell and random ions shift, cold crystals
spill through cloud and currents
surge to kiss the ground. They say

he throws off blankets, wants all curtains
drawn. I smell his burns across the hall.
Fearing, yet praising, earth's momentous will,
I wish him trust for fitful skies once more.

I say his name. I knock upon his door.

Cortney Davis, RNC

Waking

There is nothing
and then there is everything at once,
a grand re-creation.
The recovery room hums like high tension wires
or a neon sign. Go ahead, stare.
It says: *Isn't this a miracle*
Isn't this a miracle

You have returned
from that vast sleep
during which you forgot the doctor's voice.
Count backward it said,
and you obeyed, as if you had a choice
how far or to what dream you'd spin;
the mask sickening, air thin.

You slid into death's false pocket
jingled like a change
to haggle the price of a grave—
or so it seemed.
You might as well behave—
anesthesia time is a nightmare place
of thin steel hands, white-shrouded face.

Then armies of hummingbirds
buzz your veins. You hear a radio,
the clock's exaggerated tick.
You've been reborn to skin on sheets,
pain's fire doused by needle stick
The nurse's mother-face wavers before your eyes.
Waking is her truth; all the rest, white lies.

Cortney Davis, RNC

Dear Left Knee

Take this surgery as my apology,
my benediction to our ten thousand
running miles of charging pavement
and mountain hillsides, cushioning me over
boulders, frozen trails, and the all-night run
over Death Valley roads. Forgive me
for judging the world the way a knee bends.
By jolt, by jar, by quick jumps I
abused you. A man is killed for less.
Still, there was no sadness in shoes hitting
pavement. I admit I wanted my body
to be a guitar, scream high notes, float up
to rising dusk. I admit my knees were no
more than a clock's face in my mind, no brighter
than yappy dogs chasing us through downtown
streets on our runs to the mountains. Forgive me.
But damn we cursed those trails into blessings,
turned ourselves streetwise racing marathons
in American cities. No one passed us up
Heartbreak Hill. How you flexed and grinded.
You had more knee grind than winter had snow.
All your bruises spread like broken words no language
could accept. Until I watched the arthroscopic
screen, I never knew the pain that raced
through you like riptides. Sorry. You are numb tonight.
Call it Percoset holiday, knowing nothing
of polar bear-sized pain that pulses
inside your tendon. You'll like the incisions,
narrow as indigo leaves. In time we'll probe
the still earth, the reefs and volcanic ash
in our blood, in a pale gold summer,
in a moment, in a cloak of snow, in our running
world without end, Amen, Left Knee. Love, J.D.

John Davis

Sal doesn't shake

but he shuffles
trunk hunched
jaw dropped
arms swing-less and
stiff at sides
can't turn on a dime
but must stutter step
around a quarter's corners

parks n' lakes
parkson, parkinson
little lake strokes or
depression are the
doctor's three maybes he
fishes for and finally finds
when kind questions
come in company

but no help yet from
dope, dope-a-mean
I mean I mean

at poker
Sal doesn't shake
or shuffle or deal
but folds with
three-of-a-kind
parks lakes depression

at the park where
he shuffle-walks along the
row of queen anne's
lace he notices tiny
purple petals in the slight
depression at the centers;
a striking violet speck in an
otherwise ocean of flower-head
white which others
moving more
quickly easily
might miss

Richard Donze, DO

Clinic Blues for a Warm Friday in February

When warm air meets low pressure
on a philadelphia february friday
it means rain
and as the afternoon temperature
soars to a saturated sixty-six
everyone who ran for cover after
Christmas comes tumbling and stumbling
outside, crunching into rain-pummeled
snowbanks, slipping in slush
thinking spring has come
thawing blood starts and stops
then finally gets going
startled brains remember—hurt—
and have to tell somebody

Pasquale's got the crab in his back
and he's dying by ounces
Grace takes his money by the pound to
ride buses to slot machines where she
spends him a nickel at a time
when the money runs out
she'll run out
he's running out too, of
tissues and time, down to
skin and no bones, the crab took those
Grace took everything else

Pearl stopped drinking on New Year's
and hasn't felt well since
now she knows how bad it feels when
kidneys call it quits
the body fills with protein poison
and there's no booze to keep the
pain out of the brain
a year ago she was splash happy drunk in
the february rain, now she's sober and scared
and thinks she could die on a day like this

steam rises fast off hot car hoods in
slow traffic with windshield wipers
barely keeping up, the clouds hang like
so much bad news and no yellow dreams
breaking through
they'd better stop thinking about spring
because an Alberta clipper is on its way down
and this whole mess is gonna freeze up tonight
then these untimely outcomers
stirred by this unseasonable weather
will go back inside
till sometime in march

Richard Donze, DO

Awake

We may be planning a fresh start,
a promise finally to be
the model spouse and parent,
or compensate ourselves with art:
yes, we'll give up our silly jobs
perhaps as early as next year.
Meanwhile, inside arteries
fat chokes the flow to the heart.

Some day we'll finish *War and Peace*,
visit China, shout, perform Chopin,
play hide-and-seek through rolling fields
with someone we, finally, love.
Our hungry minds imagine feasts,
yet body has another calendar:
an invitation underground
arrives as the heart skips a beat.

Brain waves on a deep-sleep EEG
look like whorls of a thousand-year oak;
the archpattern flows, like variations
by Bach, written to put some
insomniac tyrant to sleep.

Awake,

no music stills our tyrant, deaf,
like T-waves rising on an EKG,
ready to strike like a snake.

Thomas Dorsett, MD

Uteri

for Mom

They were limber then
aging in the moonlight wind
swathing the hospital in Effingham
where nurses still were nuns.
Her first labor—sweaty curls inside
the leather helmet snapped beneath her chin;
his hand clacking
the motorcycle's chrome gearshift into second,
into third against the tank, dark blue,
clutching, more gas, clacking the shift knob
like a nervous obstetrician manipulating forceps,
faster, faster in '48;
exhaust pipes noting twenty miles of corn,
old milk barns, dead snakes in the dusty track
as thin as an amniotic membrane;
both cylinders hot by now, incubating;
her womb squeezing my head
one inch above the leather seat—
the reason, Grandpa always said,
the top of my head turned out so flat.
Nuns fed me whiskey from a nippled bottle
two hours after that.

I cruise inside my sports car now, windows up,
sunroof closed, move embryonic and separate
from all the pushing out there, hear
if I tilt my ear just right, the slosh
of gasoline in the tank, the rustle
of dry corn blades curling in the wind
beyond the laryngitic motor, a hiss,
a bawling calf, its mother, an occasional moan,
as I drive, waiting to be born.

Eric L. Dyer, MD

Black Lung

Cancer is a loud word
spilling over the sea like an alarm
that will not stop clanging no matter
how much water is tossed onto the blaze,
an intricate word stretching, repeating
its crude syllables like waves of oil
slicking from the coast near Durham,
near Winston-Salem, past Tampa and Havana,
through the filter tip of the Panama Canal,
then curling all the way to Valdez
and the last end-expiratory wheeze.

Cancer is a plot
told in disorganized paragraphs of run-on sentences
and awkward conjunctions, a sea story
describing a split hull bleeding
offshore toward gaping avocets and pelicans
and heavy, dripping cormorants
too far down the beach
for any government clean-up crew to reach.

Cancer is one syllable, a cough
rattling a thin figure perched on his coastal rock,
watching his own massive stern upend,
listening to the waves pound his cliff
as busy sand crabs chew dead fish,
admiring one more sunset
through the bank of his own blue smoke,
dredging one more black breath,
in no particular hurry to extinguish his fire,
to quit his stained finger play
or to reach the end of his day.

Eric L. Dyer, MD

Roadrunner

That's Roadrunner
the dropsical farmer said of Lasix, forty milligrams.
His pills were his only friends.
He gave his medicines names as if each were a pet bird.
He kept them together in a single bottle,
and their rattling became a beating of wings.

Four times a day
with thick-fingers he opened the cage
to choose an antibiotic capsule to preen
or an analgesic's sheen to display.

Once he opened the bottle too long,
and the one he called Redbird hopped out,
sat on his rheumatoid hand
and sang a mournful song.

Another time Blue Turkey,
a well-fluffed antidepressant,
escaped and flew away forever,
and the old man fell to his knees.

The little white one he called Love Bird
was a secret cure for the heart,
but he never let that one out,
and its happy song rarely was heard.

But Roadrunner, his favorite,
when loosed, dashed straight
into red beans swelling behind his barn,
looped around ascending and descending vines
a few times before streaming again, *beep-beep*,
golden yellow, like a warm canary, into the light.

Eric L. Dyer, MD

Reflected Life

Dedicated to Mitch Snyder

Newly dead, within an infinity of love,
she reflected on her life, marveling

she'd made it through that life at all
without her mind. She'd been buried in a mass

grave in Potter's Field, on Hart Island, in autumn,
when the world dreams under the firelight of trees.

Once a living woman, she'd blazed a trail
of invisibility, carefully effacing herself,

stacking her bags, overflowing with things
vital to her life, cairns on Upper Broadway.

But few people had seen her or wanted to follow.
She especially remembered her husband.

"Matthew," she had enjoyed saying his name.
They were to live together in Zurich by the lake.

He was a member of the Moscow Medical Team.
She remembered his immeasurable presence,

the silence of his hands and eyes.
She remembered the quickening peace of love.

She hadn't had a husband. There'd been no Matthew.
She could still hear acquaintances chuckling

over her absurdities. The mind failing, spirit
moves extravagantly towards itself

As a seed possesses a distinct genetics,
has the soul an ineluctable end:

an imperative magnificently to flower to love?

Susan Efird

If by Jazz

for Mark Seldon, MD

Like the rhythmic slosh over a hidden shoal,
my body gives off a prudent music,
an inner beat, pace-perfect as if
nothing had happened. Or would.
All is well, it taps with the regularity
of a grandfather clock. But it lies.
As its monotony accompanies my breathing,
I listen . . . remembering the first
flutters in my chest, the pounding burn
that invaded my neck and the roaring
throb in my ears when it seemed
my whole body rattled with percussion.

Now in control, I eavesdrop on myself.
Weather rings in my ears; dulled feelings creep
through my body. As my heart beats quietly, I listen
like a jazz lover waiting for the first note
but wary of improvisation's surprise swings. Tuned
to blood stream's sonar, I listen for anything—
any sound breaking the surface hum of my cure.
Muffled by so much care, I need to cut loose.
I want to dance, play, but fear the furtive note,
fear jazz' infectious urge, its arrhythmia and
coded scat, knowing what it will mean if
its syncopation were to become my own.

Allen C. Fischer

All That Separates

I can paralyze you with
an index finger
as effortlessly as I brush your eyelashes,
making sure you're down.
I set breaths per minute
by pressing digits in a square.
Another plunge of my finger
slides you beyond consciousness
and memory. I hope sedation lets you dream
gloriously and elusively, beyond pain,
so we can turn you,
change the dressings
where your sternum is no longer intact.
A few millimeters,
all that separates
phalanx from pectoral flap,
you from me.
Thickness worth pause.
More so, if a finger can change
outcome with the number of your breath.

Serena J. Fox, MD

Outliers

*Sadly, a scarcity of rural physicians is likely to be
a continuing feature of medicine in the USA,
even in the face of a physician surplus*[1]

Facultative anaerobes,
We
Metabolize irony
In
The frequently airless
Outer reaches.

Obligate opportunists,
We
Recognize irony
As
The bioavailable form of
Truth here.

Scattergraphic outliers,
We
Realize irony
Has
Not been shown to
Sustain life.

Yet,
We dig in.

The agar yields.

Tony Garland, MD

1. Schroeder SA. Physician shortages in rural america. *Lancet.*
1995;345:1002.

A Doctor Among Crab Apple Trees

On days I have
to tell a mother her child died
I take a walk alone at twilight,
the sun burning the earth's skin,
peeling away another day from earth's calendar.
Crab apple trees live in open fields
like latchkey children. Tulips and hyacinths
scatter their petals like tumbleweed,
the lone stalwart threatened by the quack grass
that promises to choke her, while the robin's red breast
and ebony crow wear my anger and frustration.

On days I present a first-time mother her new child,
I wake up the next morning to the sun applying makeup
to the crow's feet of the earth's face.
The crab apple trees are in full bloom—
white flowers like a sky of cirrus clouds—
and I can forgive the quack grass
for holding on too tightly to the beauty
of the hyacinths and tulips like a still devoted lover
who does not want to leave, where even the common
robin and crow's song is a duet sung in harmony.

Joseph Geskey, DO

Depression

On good days
he could sift through limestone,
a quarry of tombstones,
and parse out soil with his pen
fertilizing poems with verbs
like *rise* and *soar*, gliding
on the wings of a whooping crane
in air so pure the wind burned
flames across his face,
or walk through copper mines
in heat-furnace summer days
scraping off patina,
turning everything he touched
into a bright, shiny penny.

But on bad days,
when he would relapse
into addiction to old memories,
when the calligraphy of her signature
signed away from him,
nouns like pronouncements
waked over his body.
It was enough just
to take a shower and put on new clothes,
resisting the urge
of even this simple task,
when all he wanted
was to follow that crane into the sky
for as long as his wings could carry him.

Joseph Geskey, DO

The Chief of Medicine

Anton Steiner sits behind a rosewood desk
in the ivory tower across the street from
Armageddon. I stand before him, buck private
intern, drenched in sweat and grime after
48 hours of emergency duty. He demands
a bill of lading; handwritten cards on seventy
Brooklyn souls in various stages of entropy.
As if I had just disembarked from a European
trip, brightly colored postcards following
obediently in my wake. He has not seen
seventy humans spread like a mosaic beneath
stethoscope and rubber-gloved hands. I want
to say, I am fatigued and my feet ache, that
I don't give a damn for documentation, that
I want to sleep and shower, the way he did
before work. I want to say, the cards will not
tell Jose Martinez's story, how he died in
my arms, a steak wedged in his windpipe. How
my own esophagus quivers on the verge
of spasm. He listens impassively as dust,
the metal of his eyes dead as glacial blue.

He has forgotten the feel of membranes, slick
in a split-open chest, putrefaction from an addict's
abscess, the *all clear* shout before paddles
convulse a skewered heart. The cards will not
say why Dora, bag lady from Flatbush, thinks
I am her reincarnated son from Jerusalem, will
not recapture one iota of my pleasure when
I cut through Amber's pantyhose to reveal
the glistening head of her newborn son. Or
horror of a man who screwed himself with
a light-bulb, forgetting glass is fragile. I want to
tell Steiner these cards are old news, that
the ink was spilled hours ago, that the ink
ran like blood to my knees and elbows, that
the world is strangling in ink and paper,
that electronic patterns on oscilloscopes
are something we have invented to remove
us from matters of the heart. He says, in
mellifluous voice, the report is due by nine;
my future depends on it, that is all.

Arthur Ginsberg, MD

Sound View

Mr. Michener dies tenaciously
  in the hospital bed. Cancer
has eaten his ears to nubs. Stroke
  has pilfered his words. Eyes
brim with the justice of hemlock.
  Right hand flails like
a beached flounder, pulls nasal tube
  urgently as a deacon sounds
belfry chimes in an emergency. He
  cannot see the sound view
from the misted window, how water
  spreads like curls off shore's
chest, runs like blood in ebb tide, distills
  into sky, re-births from the plump
ovulation of clouds. He is not ready for
  the legend of white light at tunnel's
end, squeezes hand in search of intimacy.
  Eyelids droop with the effort of
not finding words, saliva weeps at mouth's corner.
  My mumbling disintegrates on
butchered ears; how can I know this passage? When
  grandsons arrive, a half smile plays
across paralyzed lips, death molds face
  placid as the sea, breakwatered past
the spit of land called Point-No-Point.

Arthur Ginsberg, MD

Bogdan Vuksanovich

At Interlaken, I push off on skates,
a rhythmic glissando across the water's
frozen meniscus. Wind works the high
branches of the birches, beseeching
sap's return. Earlier today, I wore my

instructor's cap, watched Vuksanovich
lurch from his wheelchair, weave on broad-
based legs to the examining table. Medical
students gawk at him, a zoologic exhibit,
ooh and aah, when I show them damage
according to the textbook: how eyes ricochet
like bullets, and ankles pump like a startled
deer at stroke of the reflex hammer. Signs of
assault on flowering brain, petals stripped
off matrix of tectum, tegmentum and pons,
weevils punching holes in hippocampus and
corpus callosum. I revel in this showpiece of

pathology, pull out a slick word for impaired
coordination, *dysdiadochokinesia*. They copy with
zeal, pelt questions like hard balls at a catcher.
One student blurts out, can he get an erection? We
are shamed. Bogdan retrieves a photo of his year-
old daughter. We admire shining cheeks and tiny
puckered lips. By the boathouse, ice is cracked

and heaved, a tented jigsaw, defiling geometry.
What is broken by nature has beauty, creaks and
groans like human disease. I balance on one foot,
aware that a slip could fracture bones. How we take
for granted, God-given gifts until they are ripped
away. I must go back to Bogdan with something
more palatable than the word, *rehabilitation*. Some-
thing to celebrate the dignity of his face.

Arthur Ginsberg, MD

Bear Mountain

An old man waits within bright walls
surrounded by the squeak of shoes,
the rolling thunder of pushcarts,
the swish stiff white uniforms,

the smell of feces everywhere.
Faceless voices echo in the
hall. *I'm dead*, they call, *Who are you?*
Then they turn and face the wall.

He curls under white bedclothes,
loses himself in their snowy drifts,
Only knows time and where he is
by food trays and the changing shifts.

His women have left him—what else
could they do? Exhausted, they move on.
You can't come home again, they say.
He nods and looks away.

It's time to sleep, and he dozes,
remembering the greening leaves
of spring, the brown fields of summer,
the bronze of autumn. *Let me dream*,

he thinks, *Let me sleep*. Doesn't eat.
The nurse in white muslin calls and
says, "He barely moves, his breathing
stalls. We must suction him, teach him

to swallow, put down a feeding
tube." "Let him die," I say. "He wants
to die." "But that is difficult
for us to do," and she shakes her

head and sighs. "But we both must let
him try" I say, and he smiles as
we come in the door, his breathing
deep as I touch his brow and lay

my hand upon his chest that rattles
deep down and sounds like death.
"Can I do anything for you?
Do you want the nurse to suction you?"

"No, none of that," he shakes his head.
"This may be the end." He smiles
again, and I clasp his hand and
he grasps mine—eyes clear like the top

of Bear Mountain after a storm.
He wants to die. The minutes troll by.
When I'm home, she calls that he is
gone, and can I let his body go?"

M. Kirk Gooding, MD

Aging Gratefully

"You are old, Father William," the young man said,
"and yet you continually stand on your head."
Lewis Carroll, *Phantasmagoria*

Ah! So you do look your age? Welcome it.
Waive the rules:
don't grow elderly, grow old.
Don't get graceful, get greedy.
Don't get delicate, get bold.
Live your age with lust.

Take your teeth out if you want to.
Don't cover your bald beauty with a wig.
Don't cream those creases.
Flaunt them: these highways on the map of your life.

So your skin's gotten thin? Love its wens and wrinkles:
mementoes to your life's commotions. You're not so firm?
Fatness is fine: sway that elegant belly,
juicy like a Botticelli.

Dance! Caper with the teenyboppers.
Oil that creak, bop that crunch.
Strut that wrinkle, rap that bulge.
Link arms, you redwoods that ride down our millennium,

your roots broadening with each weathering
season. Though your bows are bent
they are hardier than the stripling's green,
and their lengthening sights espy their targets plainer.

Why sit and wait on death?
The future's marvelously unsure.
So turn hoary cartwheels into a hundred suns.
We're all at it,
hoarding stories as we go;
and there's work for us all to do.

John Graham-Pole, MD

Breaking News

In the cancer clinic
people brush us as we seek
the sanctuary of an empty room
and visit death together.

Hi: (let me speak
only to sentence-end, not
anxious and artless, beyond
as if longer could delay it);

As my mouth opens
abandon-memories chill me,
and your real and present anger:
(I'll smile, stay light, not dodge;

You deserve that
I look you in the eye):
Karen, dying's fine, I say
(to myself what do I know?)

As you, knowing death
too well, assuage me;
you fear not dying but
doing it (who wouldn't?) in diapers.

So off you go,
share your final glimmerings out;
your grad-school money
will pay the funeral

Save for a last
letting-go-round Disney;
you'll binge too on allotting
your two-decades' treasures

(death like life
being costly: justly so,
two such precious things).
You're shy telling Josh:

I still (presumptuously)
love you; in time you'll
ride, in morphine-trails,
your last carousel.

John Graham-Pole, MD

A Poem Against an Ending

Rogny Les Sept Ecluses, France

Without circulation, in three minutes the brain begins to die.
So they placed my neighbor on a bed of ice
to stop his heart and splice good veins
around the bad arteries.

The parts of his body were tethered with dissolving thread,
and then they brought him back
out of frigid stillness to body temperature.

Today he stands on the porch of the church
looking at the eleventh-century portal
He must have looked at it a thousand times now,
the unusual white stone and Arabic arch.

This time I wonder if it is different.
I wonder if now a century does not seem a short time to him.
I wonder if in this hollow air before the spring rain
he does not feel the tangible presence

of a man standing at a church,
past the middle years of yearning,
and how the dead must envy him only
his place on earth to stand.

This spring I have watched the dead pass briefly
through the portal of the church.
Once they were simply placed in the south yard.
Now they are carried up the road to the east
where the morning sun ignites a pond and a field of yellow rape.

My neighbor says that it takes someone special
to live in the Presbytery——there are so many souls.
An urn of Roman coins was found
where our pear tree stands.

Now part of our garden resides in a museum,
the stamped faces of power worth far more
in their well-preserved strangeness.

Since winter I've heard sounds late into the night,
short chirrings like wings .
The sounds come down from the chimney or from the steeple.
It is an owl flying for prey.
If it were soul, it would need a body
to move the air—it is that simple.

I listen, sleepless,
enumerating fears and blessings,
the unconscious workings of the body,
the rustle of pulse,
the quiet house with stars of other millenniums in its windows.

Jeffrey Greene

Try to See It My Way

There will never be a Beatles reunion
as long as John Lennon remains dead.
G. Harrison

My show must go on at the VA clinic.
I may be out of hope, but they're not out of stories,
 though long-returned from Danang
with a pharmacopoeia of diagnoses
and a zoo-full of monkeys on their backs.
Oh Aimée the things I've seen.

How can we chant the weekly litany on such a day:
that life is good and yielding,
that we accept each other, damaged though we are,
that each day's minutiae creates a self-evident whole?

We can't. So instead we witness the fragile teary stuff
his girl guide is made of, on a winter day in a stifling room,
tarted-up with government-issue tinsel and garland.
It's neither a pretty nor reassuring sight to the vets,
most of them not yet graduated to a day pass.

They drink when they can get it,
eluding a dance known as the Thorazine shuffle,
hallucinate interior Mekong movies,
and hoard their meds in secret, in case all else fails.

In case I fail.
And today my failure seems carved in stone:
my failure, his murder, their sorrow and all this madness..

Aimée Grunberger

Chemotherapy

sorry can't leave just yet
two kids so little
still cry when they stub a toe
need help sticking bandaid
can't go right now
got a class reunion
book on reserve
four tickets to Vancouver no refunds

reading up on survivors
card-playing grandma number on her arm
ten-car pileup wheelchair for life
hopeless coma awoke one morning
bone-cracking tumor size of the sun

couldn't help it
teacher made me
said to lay my head on the desk
but everyone else can leave
heavy door slams
not so fast lady

I'll tell you why
for nothing that's why
for the hell of it
some number came up
so what you gonna do huh
just plain spiteful

put my affairs in order
ten notarized final wishes
now my bald skull
lonely breast broken heart
hunch over the muddy curb
in the filthy wind
no place inparticular
wait for light to change

Aimée Grunberger

If the Doctors Are Right

Then I've got to make some order
stop wasting what little is left
no more Times crossword especially
not the Sunday no more reruns
out of boredom no more boredom
no need to read a book to the end
read the last page first then return it
who's counting now who ever was

at this very minute
a lunar eclipse just like the paper said
that seems worth a look
(when will this constant weighing stop)
like a tall guy's shadow
takng out a piece of the screen
down in front you moron
last of the century in this hemisphere
good then I won't miss any
hate to think of it all going on
without me
now hear this
no more fun if I check out
no celestial phenomena of any sort

old man in the moon
looks alarmed and who can blame him
half his cheek and all his chin
in darkness a five o'clock shadow
worse than tricky dick
neighbors stand on their decks
all of us with binoculars and bathrobes
night is warm moon is shrinking
waning light upside down in my eye
and me standing here among them
even if the doctors are right

Aimée Grunberger

On Remembering a Small Boy's Why

Father,
I sit where willow whips
Hang limp in cool air, remembering
Old heat and whys, a palimpsest
Of fails and falling short, of splintered panes
And rakes left out of doors and peas
I could not eat and attitudes
I could not name and ands and fors,
Because of and consequence
Of doors shut fifty times for slams
And merely being where your foot
Was going, of asking when your mind
Had not come home from days of hanging
Wallboard over years of whys
Of your own. You needn't scold me
Now I confess it all, and as you said,
I hated peas because you loved them.
You made a damnable god.
I made a damnable son.
I wanted to say "God,"

                              but not to you.

I wanted to say, "God, damn you,
You have his face, the hard-muscle bulge
Of his jaw, dark eyes fearing
Behind the glare of his glasses
I cannot see you behind that stare."
I wanted to say, "God, damn him,
He steals-your place; your will is hard-pressed lips
And two hands, calloused slapping at my ears
And tearing down my sweet garden-temple walls."
I wanted to say, "God, take his little ones
And dash us against the stones"
Will God forgive me then if I
Cannot sing songs of innocence?
Remember O Lord my Babylon
(and he has whys of his own);
Your wind in the willow leaves
Has made my harp sing.

Kevin Hadduck

Hope

Three phone calls:
A farm wife with chest pains
Stealing her breath,
A woman with five children,
Her husband gone with her money,
A man who fears his mind,
For whom his own thoughts
And hands are strangers.
So here I come,
With a twittering gift from God,
Like a schoolboy
Bringing home a robin
Torn by a cat or a passing car.
They act grateful for this,
Put their hands gingerly
To the frail, demanding body,
To the beak constantly open,
The claws grasping at a finger,
The discomposed feathers
Of a small thing always near
Dying. I say to them, "Here.
Feed it with water and bread."

Kevin Hadduck

To a Friend in the Ward

On a slope of tundra high above San Luis,
a scar from twenty years ago still writhes
among the rocks where marmots scream.
In another year or so, fine grasses
and flowers small as suture knots
may finally close this shallow cut.
I'm amazed at such a surgery,
at the speed of nature's repairs.

They let you go with us for an afternoon.
We watched you shuffle through the park,
saw you make a slow turn at the waist
when a mockingbird took up his drill.
You walked with your arms hung
straight at your side, your ashen face
forward. You were far from there.
Your wounds, festering for thirty years,
have now begun consuming you.

Still, I am amazed by healings
when they come, at the shock they give
my disbelief. Their movement stirs me,
these god-like transmutations
of glacial ice into warm seas.

Kevin Hadduck

yet another child

one a.m. / stat call to the emergency room
race down the hall full speed tripping on
women lining overcrowded corridors
moaning / screaming refugee dialects
cadences of tropical confusion
as they labor to birth
yet another child

they bring him in from south central
another drive-by / the dispatcher says
blood-soaked uniform
all the official markings / ballistics wound trim
and filigree tattoos
broken bat left femur pointing out
towards a cheap wall clock that
never shows proper time
blood dripping on floors not yet healed
memories not yet erased / bone chips crunching underfoot

i rip off his pant leg / he'll never need these clothes again
sprinter's muscles filleted
by automatic fire / severed arteries
pump out agonal rhythms
at best his leg is gone / we code
for ten minutes / pounding / jabbing / the ritual good practice
knowing full well he was dead when he hit the door

i cross the street to grab a cup of coffee
his buddies waiting there
all in uniform / blue bandanas / raiders' jackets
sixty-five impala convertible / candy apple and chrome
baby moon hubs
its engine purring sweetly in a warm breeze
tuck and roll upholstery snow white
painted in a fourteen-year-old's fresh blood and shotgun shells
front doors left open wide

the boys and I / ready for the night

Mark S. Haendel, MD

Riding Chaucer in the Stirrups

Braced in that compromising position
(feet in the stirrups, pelvis slid forward)
my April ritual begins—
examination of the innards.
The patient should be put at ease,
and so we speak of poetry.
I haven't studied it in years,
you say, feeling for fibroids.
In fact, I can recite only one.
Let me . . . hear it, I grunt
between heavy pressings on my abdomen.
You clear your throat,
Whanne that Aprille with his showres soote ...
press and probe, press and probe
The Droghte of March hath perced to the roote,
I catch breath as the cool instrument
zooms in for a cervical smear.
And bathed every veyne, you pause, forgetting.
I joyfully prompt you, *. . . in swich licour*
You pat my tummy, indicating the exam is done.
I sit up, pull down the angel robe,
we join together in one more line,
Of which vertu engendered is the flour,

Geoffrey, my good man, meet my *Doctour of Phisik;*
in al this world ne was ther noon hym lik.

Sophie Hughes

Living Will

I hope to die of dailyness,
of a surfeit of suns and moons
of too much joy,
an abundance of family occasions,
countless chocolate sundaes.

When I reach out for the
sleep of the tired body
and the cluttered mind,
let me be.
Let me go, as I came,
unencumbered.

I have lost my way
in life many times,
but this last road is clearly
marked, and it leads
to a place I knew,
before love
summoned me to life,
millions of heart beats ago.

Alvin M. Laster, MD

Old Man in Bedclothes

Maybe you think no one is under these blankets,
just an old man who barely breaks
the swell of bedclothes in a hot
square room where the long afternoon

blisters. You think he is nearly gone from this skeleton
and these fingers that *pick pick* at the covers.
Maybe he is smoke,
on the shoulder of the mountain.
His old limbs are so mottled
and gray, they are like green baize poplars the belling
forest calls down all around him.
Soon he will be thistledown,
leaftip
or the whistle

between pine needles. Who can stop him?
His mouth incoherent: He is not
blueberries *plunk plunk* in the pail
or the cream jug beside the blue china.
He is god's breath. He is the dustbowl,
he is everything beginning.

Our bowed heads are so somber.
It seems we all are made of next to nothing,
moisture on the upper lip,
fluids in our dark
rocking parts. Soon what is left will uncouple

and lift to air.
His milky eyes focus once
before he is gone, like an old sail creaking out
to sea. Gone, like a window
opening in August.

Jeanne LeVasseur, RN

Danny Boy

Your parents lean over you like aspen trees
and the hospital room becomes a grove.
Their hamper laid open with pickles and sausage,
all to tempt you into moving, speaking,
laughing again, your mouth full of sunlight.
To see this, your mother would chain herself to an oven
and feed it with splinters of her own bones.

Your father would exchange places with you
in the car that crashed, he would be your headlights
and go before you if he could.

They come every day, sit and speak with you.
Your mother knits, your father reads the newspaper.
She has started at the cerebellum and the worsted trails
off her needles like a stem.
See the ball of gray yarn in her basket,
huddled like a brain. She is knitting webs and crannies, pia mater
and hopes your damaged mind, which flies around the room like
swallows, will come and nest again.
Your father reads out loud some clippings
you would have liked. He thinks if he reads
enough, he can change the course of history.
And you lie there, your heart valves slamming closed,

the message your body hears: Live, live!
This picnic is spread across your blanket.
They are waiting for the crows to shake themselves from trees,
or for something like sunlight on shards of glass
and the gleam from twisted chrome, to knit itself into shade.
They are waiting for you to waken,
to take a peach into your open hand and remember
how good it is to eat.

Jeanne LeVasseur, RN

The Machine

The machine
always perfect
without any flaw
performing all functions
cares nothing at all.
It never grows weary
no reason to rest
compression is constant
while moving the chest
of Mr. Montgomery
who lies in his bed.
His eyes stare
relentlessly
out of his head;
onto the ceiling
dark shadows fall
upward and downward
they drift on the wall.
Oxygen flows through
valves more alive
than Mr. Montgomery
whose breathing they drive.
Inhaling, exhaling,
his color is gray
the machine washes wasted
corpuscles away.
His muscles lie flaccid,
red lips are now blue,
while no one is noting
both eyes are askew.
The machine knows no limit
no visible goal;
pistons slide silently
out of control
forever recycling,
but no word is said.
With nobody knowing
Montgomery is dead.

Don Lewis, MD

Poetry of Li Bao Nguyen

(after initial exploratory surgery)

When the summer days were hot and round
With soft syrup running edges
My father took an ax
And split open the watermelon.
A cool puff of wind rushed from inside.
It was the demon of winter coming.

Now I am split open
Red and crisp,
Riddled with black seeds of cancer
And a demon that will not escape.

(during her first round of chemotherapy)

Outside my window
The street is blossoming with umbrellas:
Yellow and striped and black and red and
Black and black and gold these flowers
Each with an umbrella flower spike pointing up
To puncture the sky.

How thin everything is
The clouds that hold back the sun
The umbrella petals that hold back the rain
The window glass that holds back the street
And my eyelids that hold back the tears.

(before a peaceful death)

There is a silence inside me
Like the silence of a nest at night
Waiting for something to come alive
In a small way.

My hands are paintbrushes.
My hands are speaking in colors.
My heart is whiter and more precious than any egg
trembling to fly.

Susan Lyon

Morning Report

Standing at attention
in the damp dawn
of my novitiate
I take down
everything I need to know
about his deteriorating condition—
scheduled labs and consults
the machines and their quirks
the tubes, meds and procedures that
please God will keep him alive,
at least through my shift.

But nothing of what I was told
has prepared me for what I find
in the hectic clutter of bedsheets—
a man,
a small man
with rheumy eyes
and sleep-creased cheeks.
I stand watching, drenched in unease.
Wait! He stirs
slowly at first,
then jerks a shaking hand
from some hidden fold.

Bang! You're dead,
he says with a grin
through cracked lips,
trigger-finger leveled straight at my head.
I snap to life at this morning report
and the burden of dread falls away.
Face to face with vitality
still venting itself from
this body of death,
I am struck by the force
I must reckon with.

Veneta Masson

The Promise

If you could just lose weight
your blood pressure would go down
your diabetes would clear up
you could get off all those pills you take
your joints wouldn't ache
you could climb the stairs
run after the bus
carry the groceries
pick up the baby
the swelling in your legs would go down
you could reach all the way to your aching feet
you could breathe again

You could find clothes to fit
get out of your slippers and into real shoes
who knows but what your old man would come back
you'd get more respect from your children
a decent job
your son would kick drugs
your daughter wouldn't get pregnant again
you'd live to see your last one grown

Your neighbors wouldn't talk about you
the toilet would flush
the roof wouldn't leak
there'd be food enough at the end of the month
they wouldn't cut off your check
jack up the rent
you'd hit the number
go off for two weeks in Aruba

Jesus would save the world from sin
those who mourn would be comforted
the poor would enter the Kingdom of God
your hunger would be filled.

Veneta Masson

Heart Attack

I take my collars to the wash, dump them
and the sloshing starts. I settle back
in a plastic chair and nod, rhythm of water
floating away the day the barbed wires tight,
the grinding windmill gears I fixed. I'm lost,

alone in town at midnight without her,
in a Laundromat. I cock my head
and see two empty rows, a dozen washers closed
like portholes on a ship. I've had enough
of cruising bars with boyhood friends who always

stayed out late, but now turn off the late news
early and hug their wives at home.
My wife's been gone too long, his doctor
and teams of nurses slaving to save her dad.
His pulse, thank God, is back to normal,

that muscle tough as a bull's. I remember him
standing guard when we drove off at night,
backlit in the door, holding his glasses.
He never waved goodbye, not till we tied the knot,
a father who took all duties to heart.

When the rumbling steel machine stops,
my work clothes tumble and plop. Shoving up,
I feel my fingers numb, tingling
like when his big fist squeezed my hand
like a son's before the honeymoon.

Walter McDonald

Transplant

Old heart
Old Coyote heart
Obstinate bag of blood
Its again
Again
Swept avenues of cells
Flung in fistfuls through
The shuddering root
A beat and its chances
A beat and its chances

Old dilated bag of heavy-hearted blood
Old beaten heart, too-injured heart
Its equinox
Its limp toccata
Released tonight

A Heart's in the air!
Some kid . . .
Bleed in her head, sounds like . . .

The blade already through the root
A bay of blood in the empty chest
The fast sun sucked like a coin
Into the pocket of a thief
And the heart not yet out of the reckless sky

A trick fixture of the blood
Spilled into her burning head
The gold horn broke from her lips

Just like that.

And the heart that put jazz on the empty table
Hung like a bell in an empty hall
Fierce, muscular, resonant
In the pacific interspace between grief and prayer

The wheels kiss the landing strip
Over and over
Between beats

It ends; begins
The center holds

Dawn McGuire, MD

Thoughts of a Nurse
Returning to the Base Camp at Cu Chi

Do you remember
where the road turns right
by the graveyard
near Cu Chi?

Do you remember
the smoke of firefights
foretelling medevacs
that brought young bodies
wrapped in blood
and the filth of paddy fields?

Do you remember
the strength of my hands,
their silent love for you,
as they unwrapped
gaping mouths of rifle wounds,
cleansing and embracing
when there was nothing else to do?

Driving today
where the road turns right
by the graveyard
near Cu Chi,
I saw you then
as you lay in my arms,
child-lover,
in those moments we were alone
before they said
what I already knew.

That I had lost you,
like others lost before,
that you had left your mother-lover,
strong and firm of hand,
soft-breasted
as I held you close
to whisper
—*I won't forget you.*

Robert S. McKelvey, MD

Ode to a Parasite

I am pregnant with your work. Have you
bicycle pumps, air compressors?
You inflate me like a dirigible.

Around your diligence my belly
grows to excruciating roundness.
What combustions do you practice?

I see you with a Seuss-style sucker,
like the trumpet of a Rumpledinker
or a Heffelhumper, pink, maybe purple.

You multiply with indecency.
Your progeny wring my gut with their antics,
I, the unwilling nurse, bloated nursery.

Busily you make microscopic lace
of my lower digestion, hardly hesitate
to sew my gut to my spine.

Must you turn me inside out this way,
expose our little private struggle
to the world? People ignore us with

embarrassed courtesy, like fighting lovers.
The boyfriend complains of our relationship.
Must you respire so ardently?

How long have you traveled as stowaway
in this pressurized luxury jetliner,
clinging to its turgid walls?

And your home before this palace?
A conspiratorial faucet?
A toothbrush, partner in a third-world

ambush? You're as old as evolution.
I send to you my emissary,
a small bitter pill.

Tamra L. Myers

The Lighthouse Keeper With Stargardt's Disease

In place
of darkness there was just
dark
scars of storms burnt through
his Peyne's Grey lens
see-through and stinging as
jellyfish
stitched
to his salt-stained eyes,
and the doctor's searchlight
swept
from side to side.
She sits
in the waiting room and pretends
to read tattered years' old magazines, remembering
a young couple, fifty years behind,
in Asuncion's autumn cold, and how
he woke her, reading
Fröding's *Splashes and Rags* and a pillow
washed carelessly
with candlelight and avalanche-lillies that swept
from side to side.
He is blind, now, and cannot see her crying as
she walks him home, reminding him
of ships he's saved from Port Sable to
Cumberland Sound. She holds the pressed
Transvaal daisies up close to his eyes, sent
by a sailor who almost ran aground but was saved
by his warm light that swept
from side to side, and he pretends
to see them. They are home.
She holds his hand and love is this; he falls asleep and
she will not leave him and will always keep him warm,
and he dreams he sees her blue eyes unstung by storms.

Michael O'Reilly

Sixth Floor Lounge, Oncology

The bright globes above the park are fruit
too big for the basket, plumped with the hot
air of conceit. They skim the treetops just
out of reach of the eyehook that could snare
them from the picture window, moor them
above the sixth floor like a hope. The few kids
who visit strain to see the bright suns swallowed
by the trees, the hot breath smothered and immured,
the big fruit finally wizened like a prune. Then,
apart from the seagreen of the park, there are only
the wellworn chairs and couches, the dun walls,
the Coke machine, the banks of elevators
elevating the sleepless ones, the angry ones,
resentful the flesh of what they love has failed
them and that this place or someplace like it
is the only game in town. But what amazes
is how polite they all are, these strangers,
these absolute strangers, who confide only
in science or in God. In Intensive Care
belief is a window small as where the surface
breaks above an endless dream of water.
The inmates are ice-white, long of bone
as the neardead in the death camp
photos. And there is always a lonely hope
in the air, like a plane overhead that's one
of ours, and they know we're here.

Lee Passarella

Recovery

It's better not remembering that weekend
when "medical" and "science" didn't seem
to fit together, when medicine lurched
between the well intentioned, the inquisitorial.
Every room full, they stuck you in Recovery
far from recovered, not even diagnosed
yet. I came to you down the hall where
the operatories were, with their bloodless
tables, their big lamps in dark clusters,
the darkened monitors that had the suggestive
menace of disuse. Found you with the cut
and drugged ones on their litters, each one
swollen as the three-days drowned, faces
in a mist of oxygen from the plastic collars
strapped to them. The nurses started IVs,
strung the bags, screwed the stopcocks
hypnotized by green phosphor, as if crazed
speed were the only thing that life inhered in.
Maybe it did. They had you on medication
that left you a maze of nerve ends. Your skull
stung with the electrodes, they told you to stay
still for an EEG, your limbs imploding, tears
just at the edge of brain and eye; I felt
helpless as someone visiting Bedlam.
Later, when they found a room for you,
you got a little rest. From the doorway,
I admired those undangerous curves I
like so much as you lay above the covers,
the satin pink pajamas startling as hyacinths.
The brutal charity of hyacinths, or any
flower, in a place like that.

Lee Passarella

What Is Lost

> . . . everywhere and always,
> go after that which is lost.
> Carolyn Forché, *Ourselves or Nothing*

When she came across the border
she had no shoes only one black
Cambodian skirt, a thin blouse, the long
scarf they used for everything, sleeping,
bathing, carrying food, wrapping
the bodies of the dead.

She no longer wants to say
what happened to her husband and brothers,
afraid if words bring them back,
along will come the soldiers.

What do I have, she asks,
to keep the nightmares away?

Next to her guttural vowels
and clipped consonants, my English
strikes a tin note. The interpreter
translates my advice, and I wonder
which sound was *nerve*, which
was *heart*, which *grief.*

I give her another pill to try.
Perhaps with this one
she will sleep well
tonight. A sleep untroubled
by dreams, by memory.

She listens politely, smiles
a thank you: her only English.

Yet as I watch her leave
I know her cure comes Tuesday afternoons
when she joins the circle
of other Khmer women to sew.
Punctuating the fabric
with yellow thread, binding her remnants
into a piece that will hold.

Peter Pereira, MD

Styx

Crazy as the Devil's bedbugs,
reviler of Jews,
would-be assassin of kings:
you came in "q. 3 months"
for feeble doses of Thorazine,
the upper limit fixed
by your mystic numerology.
You changed your name
to "Styx,"
the dark-most river of Hell,
and had it blazoned
on your Medicaid card.

Three harsh years
you pressed your case
with me; how the Dean
had passed you over
for department chair—
another Semitic conspiracy!—
despite your scheme
to transmute coal gas
into gold.
You sent me letters signed,
"Styx and Stones
will break your bones,"
and swatted down my words
like bubonic fleas.

When I told you
I'd be leaving soon,
you grew ungodly still;
then, with the shudder
of some creature
poised to molt.
said, "I'm quite horribly ill,
aren't I?"
and grabbed your coat.

Where in my "mental status"
do I note
how your dark flower
opened
one frail moment.
then deftly closed.

Ronald Pies, MD

Spell-check for a Blighted Fetus

In my laptop's lexicon,
   there are no words
for your body's chaos—
   each lesion in my write-up
is searched back to normalcy.
   "Mitral" scans
as *mistral*,
   that cold, sere wind
off southern France;
   "dysmelia"
comes up *dismay*.

In these quick, cool chips,
   catastrophe is sent
to finishing school:
   "agyria" becomes *agile*,
"teratosis" goes to *tearoom*.

Poor remnant:
   if only
in your first fission
   some godly processor
had blessed
   your blighted genes;
rewritten
   their scattered base-pairs
in lucid script.

Ronald W. Pies, MD

Tracks

Once sized for subsidies,
mostly black, mostly skinny, mostly

children line the clinic halls.
The children can't see rails spreading

beneath their feet, those steel connections
feeding outer Dubuque to inner Cleveland,

all Enid to Orlando. Neither can they see
beyond these walls——to Oklahoma,

summer sand burying the plank house, its family
shrunken, alone. And, over there, Montana,

potbellied and quick, a chill rattling among the pines,
leaving them bitten, done. Behind them isn't that

Dallas, the wire line dipping, dungarees strung?
There, it must be school's first day, because down

the block, bells buzz, charged voices rush
before a loud static slows, as if someone

heard some shots and talk, they say,
is of a showdown. And in Detroit,

the Little Engine That Could replugs its cheeks,
tagged to empty before Phoenix, there to reload

leftover cheese, too many stops, too little time
to gauge the gullies or estimate the odds.

All about this tangled land engines rumble,
dust piling, bridges listing, and chickens turning thin.

And here the line crackles with tiny fires, kids
popping sparks, their green wood barely burning.

Count it all, the cored cotton bud, the combine
and chain saw, the pilfered engine parts——

with maids from proud tobacco halls
sweep the trashed receipts from courthouse steps,

grab what's there and paper the walls
with all that's lost. Run the ledger's tall columns

until it's clear—the sum is nothing
and all that's left is unmeasurable heat.

Rafel Dwaine Rieves, MD

Arlington Cemetery

General Lee's garden:
purpled shoots rise;
jackets open, kids
race down the paths;
tombstones settle in
snow melt and March wind.

Stone crosses parade the slopes:
soldiers fallen in battle
or faded in nursing homes.
Snow highlights graves
with translucent peace.

Kennedy's eternal flame,
fire blue and gold,
burns flanked by cameras.

Tall soldiers with shined brass
stamp, black shoes click heels,
change arms, honor a rock box,
Tomb of the Unknown Soldier.
Skulls and armbones tumble,
souls riding the gusts.

We tromp to the ridge
where physician soldiers lie,
surveying the Potomac.

Walter Reed rests here,
"Conqueror of Yellow Fever"
enabler of the Panama Canal.

General Rumbaugh died
parachuting into Honduras,
airdropping a hospital.

I remember: bugles calling Taps,
sharp rifle cracks,
the long line of mourners.

His epitaph: "He did not
merely exist in our world; he
roared through it, carrying
the rest of us in his vortex."

The breeze blows, flags snap.
So many grieve here.

Next, we seek my grandfather:
small headstone with Russian
cross. He fought in three wars,
and died at 85, demented.
No tourists.

Daffodils spurt upwards.
More bugles sound.
Trees dream of bloom.

Elspeth C. Ritchie, MD

Korean Birds

Yongsan Army Base, Seoul

In the land of the morning calm,
the evening din is raucous.

Blue and black magpies squawk,
quarrel for sticks to festoon bulbous nests;
trains burrow underground,
helicopters churn overhead.

An asylum of my parent's America
survives on this military base:
school girls swing hands,
men tend grills of flamed burgers,
wives shop for peanut butter.

Long barrels hover
thirty miles north,
steel egg shells of
nerve-blocking gas,
threatening to hatch carnage
and drop a sea of fire.

When my father served here,
pulled from college in 1952
to decrypt communist codes,
trees were stumped by shells,
rubble and white crosses.
No bird song.

Plants and birds now
rise hopefully, but
old Koreans still walk
bent and bowed,
frail from a childhood of
tank-scarred rice fields.

Proud grandchildren riot,
pour kerosene on
stronger bodies
(flaming, falling)
to reunite their
divorced mountain land.

At the army hospital
we play war games,
plan for mass casualties,
give orders in gas masks,
file with flashlights
into the bunker built by
Japanese conquerors.

Ring-necked pheasants,
red, green and gold,
strut about our barracks
like arrogant generals.
They call cadence on my roof,
eat bread crumbs I scatter,
scuttle at choppers.

We have one pilot dead,
one captured up north.
What birds does the
living man hear?
Magpies battling to tear
at his dead friend's eyes,
or golden pheasants
crying to mate again?

Elspeth C. Ritchie, MD

Pumpkin Flowers

Yellow blossoms glow
between large fans of
leaves. Vines spill
past nasturtium bounds
into the shaggy lawn.

I should mow, weed,
neaten my unkempt Eden.
But pumpkin tendrils
grab the passive grass,
strangling out sun.

Morning glories ride
my fences, violet
blossoms radiating dawn,
spreading sunrise up
into the tree above.

Their heart-shaped leaves
tangle the baby tomatoes;
I snip their life lines.

How do you choose between
the flower and the fruit?

A young tulip poplar
shoots up straight
shading golden mums.
Too close to my home,
his roots threaten bricks.
Finally, I chainsaw him down.

In therapy I also dig,
scoop at resistance or
rake memories towards the dawn.
I edge the boundaries on
the psychiatric ward,
locking doors,
granting passes,
keeping blades away
from soft untended arms.

In an herb garden,
stray tomatoes become
weeds to be pulled,
so dill can wave green
feathers at the sky.

May my hands fertilize
medicinal leaves,
sweet berries and
glory-giving blooms.

Elspeth C. Ritchie, MD

Postcall

Postcall you come home diminished, wan, your hands
faltering at the lock. You feel a need to tell me
each patient's history before you sleep,
the progress of each malignancy, the way the family
spoke to you, the suffering that makes death a release.
I understand. But I wait for you, Isabelle,
not your stories of the progress of the dying.
I lead you to bed like a child, almost crying
with fatigue and despair these anaemic mornings
when you have donated all your strength
and then come home to me, stricken, empty
and grateful for the smallest gesture of tenderness,
my easing your heel from your boot as you undress,
holding you while you try to reclaim your membership
as one who sleeps. Your limbs twitch
like a dog's, hurrying into dreams, your lips
part with sighs. I soothe you with my weight,
whisper about the snow piling up outside.
Your eyes close, it's late afternoon, slow repose
beckons. But even in dreams your fingers pleat the quilt
as if gathering the flesh of an arm before a shot.
I understand. Accountability never leaves your hands.

Rachel Rose

Sleepwalker

The first time, so they say,
I cut the heads off a row
of Mother's lilies and cast
white petals to their sister stars.
When Mother woke me on the swingset,
I peed and was led back indoors.
Easter time, I collected imaginary
eggs in an invisible basket: hung
on my arm like a purse. My palm
remembered the fragile weight
and plucked a pink one nesting
in my parents' covers. Father lay
quiet, his mouth open, like
a soldier struck dead. At twelve,
they say I carried pails of sand
to the edge of the pier, back
and forth, until a sand castle
perched above the busy waves.
After that, my parents nailed windows,
solved complex alarm kits for doors,
and tied a string around my ankle,
spooled to a bed on their headboard,
tying me to wherever they go in dream.
Tonight, the house is dark.
They are still asleep.
The boat goes mad
as I lower my net
into the deep.

Caryn Russell

Felt Image

That's silly. I feel whole. No
goodbye kiss? No gratitude for
the luxury of a perfectly fitted
shoe, for touch, for the clasp
of prayer? Yes, it would be crazy.
You, Doc, out digging in the snow
with a tongue depressor. Yes,
my hand, my leg were parts, not me.
But where are they? Where did I go?
I am here, not wrapped in linen in
the dark. The bathroom mirror stills.
I bob like a dead fish, breath caught
in my carcass. Doc, my phantom leg
folds through the bed. While asleep,
the nurse stuck on somebody's fist.
I don't think it will ever open.
It's a forty pound balloon. Half
of everything is gone. Look,
the dock only has twelve through
six. Is pain a referred opinion?
Can it totally push me out? Why
should I glove a hand that is not
mine? I ask you to pray for me.
You say you will, but I'm not sure
you believe, or will remember.
After you leave me, the fire burns
down to a watery place where you've
cushioned me until dawn. Shhh. Shhh.
"Yes," a voiceless voice says to me,
"Forget you are tethered to this bed.
You are not a boat in its slip. Step
into the weather of your health. Hear
lightning behind the eye. Inside,
night illuminates with knowledge
beyond what you feel or can ever
understand. You——are——not——lost."
Constellations of cells converse,
course their way through darkness.
Listen, Hear them speak to one another,
Yes, yes, I am more than this.

Caryn Russell

AIDS In Haiku City

I

Bravery and waste:
his beauty breaks new ground. One
golden leaf drifts down.

II

Spectacular as
peacocks his defenses failed
closing rainbowed tails.

III

Hands of ginko trees
reshape identity's torn
shroud to fluted fans.

IV

Our losses rise with
temple bells as mourning cranes
call, circle, and fall.

B. A. St Andrews

AIDS Test

Don't think of the hand holding the needle—
think of the needle itself, its flesh

glass and familiar, vacuum-solid
and thirsty inside. The skin becomes

permeable as beachhead, yielding
into grains and open space. You are liquid now

and moving, drawn to emptiness
by emptiness expanding.

What they take from you
is future, desire drawn into itself

in the warm blue runnels of blood
which climb the needle, gush

red, formlessness
approaching form, the shape of desire

traveling away from you, captured, answerable.

Ellen Samuels

Queen of Buzz

Cold cameo, my stethoscope's full moon
Fades. Then's shed this shard of skein, sprung pyx
Of snow-thin wafer words, unstruck bells of the brow—
Clotted, toxic alluviations of Styx.

O beautiful bather, the ship in the bottles
of IVs unhinges. The cold waves the hull
Hanging by, her documents jettisoned, her lifeboats,
Her cold coral cache inviolable.

The crash room shrieks stillbirth unmercifully.
Pearls of great caprice sting in poppy hail,
Scintillations of this fiery fuselage reentering
Itself from the oracular side of parallel.

O flutterer gnashing your plumage on the altar
Of the amphitheater, O priestess racking your entrails—
My coat spiculated in the rime of midnight ritual, thrashing
In the netting of my nerves, I flail and flail

For the trapeze of your wingspread. Agonizing the burgeon
Of burden mouth-to-mouth, your last kiss I presume,
While the lost continent of the sun, gored guerdon of islet
Stars, stones with the full moon your imperfect tomb.

Charles C. Sanders, MD

Body Language: 5 East, NIH

His feet punctuate
an awkward story,
drag-dropping commas
perpetually, but
never periods, while
white coats and clipboards,
attending, up and
down the corridor,
attempt a literal
translation, his body
to the page—but how
to render the suspense
of a contraction,
how to elucidate
large muscle plotting
against large muscle,
how to retain
the style of a writhe,
how to exegete
infinite motion,
here, where there are
no edits (no one
knows how) and his
dystonic sentence
runs on and on.

Barbara Seaman

Hospital Gown

Maze.
Mop.
Unsealed envelope.

Conformist whose ties
to reality
are at best tenuous.

Gauche, careless,
broad-minded to a fault
Closet comedian

whose neckline hangs
a lopsided grin,
whose wrinkles linger

like a grimace. Thin
curtain. Backward U turn.
Cloud of cloth with sleeves

like faucets. Wash
& wear history.
Pre-fab soul who is

whisker-short,
pro-life, pro-shift,
versatility on legs.

Giver.
Taker.
Blue apology.

Barbara Seaman

Red Cross Orthopedic Hospital, Kabul

White light bursting through a volley
of narrow windows. Backlit, five men benched,

khaki-skinned, a rubble of beards, one graying.
Eyes like caves, and for the everlasting

length of one shutter click
they stare at me. I stare back at five

unmatched pairs of legs lined up like columns
of newsprint in two different languages.

Right   right   left   right   left
are boned, fleshed, juiced, blood-warmed.

Left   left   right   left   right
shoulder-strapped, hinged, a riveted

prosthesis bare to the hip, on the end of each
thin strip that runs from knee

to floor: a shoe skewered like a kabob.
How to speak two languages at once.

Five men learning, a sixth sitting apart
in shadow, his unmatched pair dangling

mid-air. All of nine, he doesn't look at me
but stares instead at practice pairs

of footprints glued like a path
to the hospital floor. Bold yellow feet,

they strut across page thirty-six
left right left right out of the picture.

Barbara Seaman

Forsythia

He was there, at the end
of the passage, his door shut,
eyes closed. On our first visit
we found this: the old man,
a baker, now crust, unable
to weep for his dead wife,
sat in the room where
the air was tongue-thick
and dark as a closed mouth.
No customers came, no family;
there weren't cakes
for celebration or sale.

In time he said something to us
but in the dark: his words cracked
and crumbled, scattered
from the slightest breath
into the darker corners.

Then, when we came: the door
ajar, he mumbled into the darkened gap.
Then, sometime later: we saw
a yellow light that spread
from door lintel to the floor
of his room. He was there,
looking out to the forsythia
spreading its yellow light
beyond the walls. He spoke,
each word intent for branch
and for flower.

James Sedwick

Outpatient

Synecdoche: a trope, or figure of speech,
in which the whole is called by an aspect or a part.

To the clinical subspecialty
that might be called Synecdochy,
I'm a cough. I've announced myself
to the back on the next bench
who stiffens noticeably. His missus,
oblivious, thumbs a worn-out *Life.*
The lab coat behind the counter
has me as a number, not the next.
Me, I know what to do & I'm doing it.
I've been a phone call, an appointment
a registration. Now, I'm an examination,
an x-ray, a chest. Nothing new:
I've been a head, a seat, a return.
I've been a protest before, an abstention,
I've been a nay. I can be an absence,
a withdrawal, a checkout, a resignation,
a vacancy. . . .

Henry M. Seiden

The Half Born

I have seen the half born—
the ones who are not wholly here.
They wait behind the mirror of memory:
Holding themselves for another world.

Elena has taken a boat,
she is rocking on an inland sea.
Bobbing through those dark eddies:
She is hiding.
Fish are her companions and birds
that circle this inward sky.
No one else can find her.

Sara is coming undone.
Her soft body unwinds silently,
like ribbon floating off a spool.
Do not try to stop her:
She is traveling—almost home.

Nicole has chosen an arctic death.
Her limbs are glaciers—
blue and luminous they shine
in the polar light.
No one can track her
across the frozen tundra:
And she will not turn back.
She is vanishing without grief
her dark eyes fixed,
opaque, the intensity of ice.

Gail Shafarman

Tinnitus

All night the woman floats
in her twin bed, hearing the wind
whoosh, the rain slap and beat
against shutters. She has given
everything to find this white river,
where she can stand and see the glacier
move its snout along a ridge, nosing
the ground as it uproots trees and sends
rocks to their death.

But rocks can't die, she thinks,
as wind and rain pour ceaselessly
through her. She supposes the past, like matter,
can be neither created nor destroyed.
And as she sleeps she rummages through
shells on a beach, touching feathers
that murmur like birds, looking
for her lost ring. In her dream she hears
the common crow chase a red-tailed hawk
into a corner of the sky.

Beside her bed the ocean roars
its single name, coursing from the sound conditioner.
A light rain thrums, wind choruses
its white noise. Deep in her cochleas
she hears her mother's fine china
shiver from a shelf and break.

Judith Skillman

End Stage

My brother rises from his easy chair,
staggering as the darkness follows him.
The soles of his feet feel nothing at all
but he has learned how to embrace the air
and sway across the rhythm of his heart.

As his movements loosen, time falls apart
till he finds himself braced against the wall.
His steps have shrunken with his sight and there
is little he can follow beyond the dim
edge of hope that leads him down the hall.

His barefoot shuffling is the sound an old
man makes but he will never get that far.
Now he would settle for the bedroom door
and a slight breeze from the open window
that tells him where he is and nothing more.

He enters a shaft of light and turns gold
for a moment, his skin glowing as though
radiant with warmth. Yet he is always cold,
growing paler as the day wanes, and light
no longer makes a difference. At night

when childhood is the center of his life,
memories and dreams are the only sight
he has. There is something he wants to know,
he says, something important that we are
missing. I listen, knowing he is right.

Floyd Skloot

Oncogene

Before eyes, before eye color, before
fingers, before breath and cry, it was there.
Nothing to be seen or touched, something more
like a current, a stirring of the air.

When he stood by his desk in second grade
muttering through the pledge of allegiance,
it was there. At ten, the first time he played
cello solos before an audience,

it was there. A readiness in the cells,
an occult passion for growth. When he dreamed,
it was there as the secrets a ghost tells
while the wind shifts. In moonlight as it gleamed

through lids half open in sleep, it was there.
It was there when he ran beside a creek
at first light, taking the sharp winter air
into the soft tissue of lungs grown weak

now, though he is only forty years old,
though he was strong, though it began somewhere
deep in his bones. That day when he was told,
he already knew. It was always there.

Floyd Skloot

Rockaway

The last of morning mist lifts from the beach
to unveil snowy gulls pecking the foam line
for food. I walk out of the rising tide's
reach toward our lair of driftwood where sun
off your glasses flashes like a beacon.

Our cedar cottage through dunegrass and salal
is not where I want to be now. I belong by
the sea, at home with ebb and flow, storm
surges, and surf-gouged rock caves filling
as wind shifts. Caught in a web spun from
the full moon to a dune's toe, I crave
the aura shorelight brings to swash zones.

The island I was raised on slowly built itself
back despite losses to winter seas and hurricanes
by drawing from the gentle sand-laden swells
of summer. I remember the flattened profile
of its December beach and can smell oceanfloor
carried like a godsend on the longshore current.

This is the kind of natural healing you remind me
cannot be done alone. Behind you as I move
to softer sand, an elderly couple hugs to start
their slow climb over dunes toward home.

Floyd Skloot

Achil Island

The sound that wakes me is a shepherd's call.
Dawnlight, island wind, and a steady leak
of nightlong rain within the bedroom wall
leave me no hope of returning to sleep.
Soon the shepherd moves down to the creek,
calling as he goes, and the wind carries
a quick motif of bleats. Each day this week
the same strange concerto as he harries

them home, his solo trilling like a crazed
bird's. I listen as they turn toward the sea,
admiring the harmonies though my days
have been tuned by chance to another key.
I remember what it felt like to be
running alone in early morning light
by the river's edge and suddenly see
a flock of Canada geese taking flight,

startled as I appeared around a bend.
Six years have passed, but I can remember
feeling so buoyant that I could pretend
to skim over land like a bird in air,
arms out, honking as I leaped for joy where
the river spread itself over the falls.
Now even dreams have stopped taking me there.
But when I hear the shepherd's morning calls

die away, it is clear the time has come
to follow him across the mountainside
past his sheep grazing among ancient stones.
As I walk down to the sea at low tide,
sunlight glitters where the herring gulls glide
and dive. When I stumble along the creek,
I am cheered by a corncrake's rowdy cries
as my cane sinks deep into the wet peat.

Floyd Skloot

Manet in Late Summer

"The exquisite creations of these last months,
when Manet was too exhausted to finish anything
more demanding, were a series of paintings of flowers."
Otto Friedrich,
Olympia: Paris in the Age of Manet

With his eyes closed
the pain is cobalt
blue flaring to brilliant
orange whenever he is
touched. There are no
black edges and no shadows
to it, only this thick
burst of purest color
in a field spread sap
green to the horizon.

All week he has tried
to paint a young woman
on horseback, a bugler,
an Amazon, anything other
than flowers. Sunk to
the chest in warm water,
he nibbles a loaf of rye
bread tainted with ergot
and swears if he could rise
tonight he would slash
his last canvases to rags
with his palette knife.

As his movements shrink
the world grows too great.
All he knows must now be
contained in two clusters
of white lilacs, the cut
flowers flaring like hope
where they rest on black.
Across the room a vase
of pinks and clematis
catches the fading light.

Floyd Skloot

Memory Harbor

No one creates. The artist assembles memories.
—Jack B. Yeats

The doctors say memory becomes
fragile in people with my disease.
The doctors say what memories
we do form are easily shattered.
The doctors say we are slow
to make decisions as the flow
of information swells. They say
we have great difficulty extracting
information from the environment.

I no longer know what to trust
when the past comes into view
like a harbor and the boat
my father pilots begins to swing
in one great arc toward the sea.
His face catches the grim
morning light and my mother
in the window of a shack turns
away from the view. Yet I know
my father was a butcher
in the city and my mother
never rose with morning light
in their whole life together.

Didn't we live by the sea
at the end and didn't we turn
away from one another morning
and night? I no longer know
where to turn when loss
like a gust of wind swings
me back again to open sea
where the sun that I knew
was a smooth disk rising
behind me grows edges now
as it sets and glows coral
and bittersweet, glows crimson
and scarlet in the moment it
sinks below the shimmering horizon.

Floyd Skloot

Since the Accident

Anomia, the inability to name objects,
is caused by injury to the inferior frontal gyrus.
The Merck Manual

Ah this, this is the thing you might pour
soup in to heat up, or water for tea.
First you have to light the flame on the box
where people cook. Those? They slip on your sox
and then you have to bend and tie them tight.
Well, with those on the lower part of your
arm, of course. Yes. A part of the body,
sure enough, you can also count with them.
Fingers? If you say so. That could be right.
I know that is happening. This notebook,
see, I draw pictures of things and then look
them up when I get stuck. It's a real shame,
but this is how I have been, day and night,
since the accident. I just lost the names
of everything. Except for butterflies,
which is what I do not understand. Why?
Nelson's Hairstreak, Swallowtail or the Bay
Checkerspot. No problem. Wood Nymph, Pine White,
the Northern Blue in a field of lupine,
California Sister——the names come out fine.
Show me a specimen; I can tell you
what it is without thinking. But to say
ankle? That is something I could not do
if you asked me to. I cannot do it.
A blank. I did? Maybe by accident,
or how I breathe. The way I still can cry.

Floyd Skloot

Autumn Equinox

I feel my body letting go of light
drawn to the wisdom of a harvest moon.
I feel it welcome the lengthening night
like a lover in early afternoon.

My dreams are windfall in a field gone wild.
I gather them through the lengthening night
and when they have all been carefully piled
my body begins letting go of light.

Indian summer to leaf-fall to first frost
the memories that were carefully piled
become the dreams most likely to be lost.
My dreams are windfall in a field gone wild

now that memory has abandoned them,
now that Indian summer, leaf-fall, first frost
have become the same amazing autumn
skein of those dreams most likely to be lost.

I feel my body letting go of light.
I feel it welcome the lengthening night,
the windfall of dreams that have long been lost
to Indian summer, leaf-fall, and first frost.

Floyd Skloot

Storm in the Morning

Stormlight and wind-driven rain weave
this morning through a warp of air.
I close my eyes against the glare
of memory but I am there
again, the place I cannot leave
for good, where light turns green and rain
hammers through air too thick to breathe.
I turn away and try to hear

last night's great horned owls, their hoots clear
in the light wind shaking the trees
they called from, but nothing remains.
I have nothing more to retrieve
except the wind and the first rain
against the window as sleep came.
There is just one place I have been
where light and rain alone can weave

such mornings through a warp of air.
To get there I pass through a sleeve
of pure dark, landing in a bare
field where I have nothing to fear
from what stormlight and blown rain weave
together through a warp of air.
But I know the dark is a cloak
that lifts to show the familiar

house, a brick street already stained
and slick with the whisper of rain.
On a morning like this I woke
to see a panel of roof eave
skewering the heart of an oak
in my yard and the ceiling stained
by grass. Glass shards winked everywhere
I looked. I know I am not there.

All I have to do is wait here.
Yes, I know I do not know where
I am now, so I must be near
the source of peace. Across the years
to this bed blazed by a long skein
of dreams, I find myself at ease.
I see where I am. In the clearing
sky the sun rises. I believe

another storm has passed like smoke.

Floyd Skloot

Old Malady

FROM the Shade of a fallen laburnum
dark with poison
you lurk,
fleet across the sun-trap clearing,
dart and silk,
jaw alert with limp rat tail,
and merge with innocent land.

Suddenly you were never there.

My astonishment is no surprise, for
I have known you, and
felt your catness. Your feline essence

falls behind me in the hedgerow as I walk.
Your gait is cerebral.
Once before I saw you, or thought so,
hinting in the hedge-gap depth
a stance, arrogance, nonchalance,
a butter-cream lick
and a spurning flick of tail

whose ninth stroke would pull me in
to the parallel path you have stalked
since boyhood.

You are not leashed to my dimensions.

Blair H. Smith, MB, ChB

Semaphore

Sometimes a word seems to fall
into an inaccessible gyrus
of my brain and is lost forever.

Then there are times it snaps back,
coursing up from a hidden sulcus,
bounding across thousands

of synapses. *Adamantine* recently
did that. Ironically, it was a word I once read
and never looked up.

Then this week—brindled, gibbous,
Rift Valley fever, Gaucher disease.
In medical school I depended on

my excellent memory. I was quick.
I gathered them in, each word
a shibboleth to be placed

in its proper quarry. Again today,
a patient I often see was in and
I couldn't remember her name,

but then a girlfriend's phone number
from tenth grade came to mind.
That's the proof. It's all there

carefully tucked away. Everything
is recoverable: agnosia, semaphore,
von Hippel-Lindau disease.

Marc J. Straus, MD

Before That

Synesthesia, metaplasia. Before that
my language was acquired on the corner of East 10th Street,
Alice Singletary lip-synching every song. Archie
Grover starting every sentence with "hey." Somehow
an occasional three-syllable word entered my vocabulary.
My tenth-grade paper was on Hemingway
and Mrs. Clara Mann wrote across the top in bold red,
"needless to say, you missed the symbolism entirely
in *A Farewell to Arms*—C minus." For the next exercise
she asked us to write a poem in class. I sat the hour
and angrily penned a dark and pessimistic verse. God
had disappeared in fear (and this was a religious school).
"This is an A plus," she wrote in red in the margin,
"but you must pay more attention to Yeats."
That may have been asking too much, but soon
I had found Rilke, Bishop, William Carlos
Williams, and Stanley Kunitz, who wrote about a slap
his mother gave him across the face when he was five
that still stung sixty years later. Words were pistols
and fireballs lined up like dominoes across a line. Words
etched out the cilia in my throat and held my ankles down.
Later, in college and medical school, language stretched
on an unending yardarm. It became convoluted and specific.
Sometimes I yearned for simplicity—Joe Applebaum
tapping the top of a garbage can—do wop, do wop;
hey everybody, just do the hop.

Marc J. Straus, MD

Autumn

Sometimes you say it's smaller. Today
you say there's little difference compared
with last week, and last week, I remember
you said it was a touch larger, and would change

the treatment. Yesterday there was a toad
outside my window after the rainstorm.
The season for flies was over and its song
was decadent. The apples have reddened

and the crabgrass has died leaving
a perfect lawn. In the early morning
the tips of the leaves have a silver
sheen. The lake behind O'Dwyer's house

has those coruscating ripples at 7 AM.
Brandon's dog is barking. The yellow school bus
pops out the stop sign and four kids climb
inside. A little one looks back. His mother's

rubbing her hands together thinking about
the day's errands. Her husband will be home
on the 6:54, open the door, lay down
his paper and fix a drink. I would touch

the lump myself to be certain
but it's already chilly out. I'll order
some logs and lay in a good supply
for winter, wondering what you'll say next week.

Marc Straus, MD

With the Dying

The afternoon lofts like a song,
this man dying fast, this one
dying slow. The words spoken here

are dust-laden clouds over fields of rice,
the rain will pour over these hospital beds
as the last words sink down and are found.

Some days the ward looks like a village
in a season of monsoon. They are leaving us
on both sides of the corridor, the man who

has forgotten his name, the old woman
whose head is sprouting lumps of cancer
like shiny, all-knowing eyes.

I come to rub their feet
like a granddaughter or a good sister
and I hold their hands and tell them

we are all worthy of this one thing,
we are all deserving and able to die.
I come to learn what they teach

about love——that it must forget itself,
must belong wholly to the beloved
and the needs of the beloved,

the muscles aching to be stroked,
the naming of the beautiful
in every mutant form.

I come to sit with the dying
because the green stalk grows in the charnel-ground,
because of love, forgiveness, and letting go.

Beret E. Strong

Ebola

1.

Today we will learn the words
for the blood's impolitic transgressions
beyond the body's boundaries.
Follow me as we travel
cephalad to caudad
over this familiar terrain.

Epistaxis describes the thin insinuations
that trickle from the nasal culvert.
Hematemesis, the sudden red gush
from a deep recess.

Next, the three elemental contaminations:
hemoptysis, blood in the wind,
hematuria, blood in the water,
and hematochezia, blood in the soil.

Menorrhagia, hematospermia:
we even name
the sad stigmata of the sexual fluids

although blood from the ear,
blood from the eye
and blood from the skin
are spoken of only in
the fastidious circumlocutions
of hagiography

and with fear of the Lord

The fourth stain
is blood borne like magma
on the body's whole fire
on the radiant and terrible
viral throng, Ebola,
unraveling the whole weave
from inside out
and beyond, beyond . . .
But that lesson's for another time.

2.

A town named
for a birdcall.

The name of a river,
as slow and brown
as its wandering water.

A field,
a perimeter of light,

(the light falls in slits
like a tattered bed net
from the bare bulb sun)

its ochre stubble
is burned to the height
of a man lying on his back.

The dull red clay is cracked
into dust and fissure
so thirsty that it pulls

the spreading black stain down
like doomed roots
around the man dying

on his back in the field
alone with the sun,
blood, stubble, wind.

No one comes near.
The world bleeds and breathes contagion,
and burns with fear.

Paula Tatarunis, MD

Gay Men's Chorus

... Heaven blazing into the head
W. B. Yeats, *Lapis Lazuli*

Here, black is de rigueur; each man fills
or does not fill his suit accordingly,
but side by side on the risers
they blur and share one elegant foundation.
Their buoyant faces float
upon a black *mare tranquillitatis*
which is also, after all, the crooked grin
of the man in the moon
before he opens his mouth to sing

as they do, now, taking
a grand unison inbreath
before the downbeat. This is the moment
before the song leaves the body,
when a narrow cage can chafe it raw,
when a ragged throat can throttle it,
and elegantly named demons—
candida, pneumocystis—
can claw at it as it struggles past
on its beautiful borrowed air.

But when it wheels, released,
into the updraft of sound
we see that even breath can be shared
into a sufficiency,
that chests can rise and fall
as if ribs were interlocked side by side
in a bellows chain—

and for a time,
the scattered attenuating faces
are translucent to such joy
and to such sorrow
that they seem angelic!
The wasted scapulae
that flare beneath rich black
seem wings about to erupt,
and the sound seems to boil up out of all of us.
Oh how we long to follow it!

But the song must fall back
into the particular body,
back into each son, lover, brother, father, friend;
must always fall back
into the warm and bloody particulars
of throat and tongue;
it must fall back like love does,
which is also lashed
to its particular body,
like a poem struggling to escape
its contingent lexicon,
and its absurd alphabet,
as if on a dare.

Paula Tatarunis, MD

EKG

A bit of saggin on your tracing, he called to say,
the STs to be specific, oh, inferolaterally,
about half a millimeter in 2,3,F and V3-6,
terribly nonspecific, as a doctor you must
see it all the time yourself; I ran it past
the cardiologist, he said don't worry—
absent symptoms, it's most likely nothing.
You *will* call, though, won't you, for any squeezing
in the chest, short breath, skips or faintness?
Good. We'll do another in a year. Just to be safe.

Take care, he said, and then hung up and left me
alone with a half millimeter of deviant electricity
sagging like crepe down my sad sack left ventricle.
Damn! I always thought my Apocalypso Now
would be announced by mammogram or Papanicolaou,
as an errant constellation stippling the webby
gamma space inside my tit, or some queer mitoses
among the exfoliated eosinophilic roses
of my cervix. If not the when, I thought I knew the how:
languishing through a long grim reaper foreplay—

long enough, at least, to see it coming,
le grand *petit mort*, the *coitam* post whose drumming
there is no tristesse, ever, nor cigarette.
But no, it could be a simple hydraulic glitch
that delivers me straight from *media res* to ditch
with no chance for confession or even for hamming
it up a bit! *Et, tu, Brute!* You seditious chunk of meat!
You pull the heist and I take the heat?
Well, lub dub to you too, bub. You bet I'm gonna snitch!
We'll both fry together when they pull the switch.

Paula Tatarunis, MD

Forensics

Exfoliations in the slits between the floorboards,
Catamenial sloughs behind the stove,
Stick a meat thermometer into her liver
While the old LP stammers *love, love, love.*

From waxy pallor to dependent purple,
the silver bullet's ricochet occults,
spattering the ontological profile,
and the fudged lab result.

Dust for double helices, uncoil the prints,
segregate the doctor from the spinster—
the missing piano wire is high C#,
the prime suspect is the minister.

Now call the chief detective's daughter—
she's playing with her Barbie on the walk.
She got an A in Art this past semester
so she's the one who always brings the chalk.

And when the house is empty as a motive,
yellow tape festooning every sill and door,
I'll slip out to pay my final homage
to your pallid outline sprawling on the floor.

Paula Tatarunis, MD

E Is for Elephantiasis

It must be 10 o'clock. Microfilariae
swarm into the hot, red pulsing streets,
into the mean, corpuscular crepuscule,
all joie de vivre as they eel and boogie
through their nightly courtship mardi gras.

Not for them these sedentary boondocks
where the lymph laps at the back stoop,
and no one goes out at night much anymore.
We were that young once, dear. Do you recall
the night we met? At that jazzy downtown dive,
oh, what was it called—Hepcat's Portal Vein!—
no hipper joint north of The Acetabulum.
Yes, we were Wucheraria bancrofti's best and brightest!
We seized the night; the whole world rigored round us.

Not that we didn't suffer. Although they say
Anopheles is a country club next to Gulag Culex
that mosquito was our love's crucible!
Recall our hasty moulting in its gut,
amidst the jeers and taunts of gametocytes
(Plasmodium malariae, we thought,
from the accent and the attitude)
and how I almost lost you in the crowd!
Then came our long forced crawl into the thorax,
and the strangling sluice down the proboscis,
back into this dear, familiar world!

You, my love, were steadfast at my side
through it all, then through exhausting weeks
of bushwhacking in the fibrillar underbrush,
where snarls of actin, ropy myosin,
dense fascial walls and cliffs of slick, brown fat
couldn't mask the inexorable dim summons
that resounded like a heartbeat in our blood.

Remember with me, dear, how, in extremis
we awoke upon a misty shore, day breaking
on a vast lymphatic channel, our fated Love Canal!
Once in our element, oh, how we flowered!
Have ever filaments burned so white hot
as we did then, or coiled so tightly one
around the other? Darling, I think not.

The rest is history. And so what's left?
The mortgage paid, the kids all off to school,
we turn our thoughts toward matters of the spirit.
The priest reminds us Sundays that each joy
has its kindred sorrow hidden somewhere,
so we've spiced our gratitude with piquant shame,
knowing that occulted in our bliss
is a black, basaltic bedrock of affliction.
And that none of it, thank Helminth, is our fault.

Paula Tatarunis, MD

Psst, Your Cognitive Slip Is Showing

Three times, lately, reaching in
the brain's dark closet for "wardrobe"
I've pulled out "vocabulary."
Seems mind has grown a temperamental lobe.

Well, OK, both concepts *do* express,
and each clothes a certain nakedness
but I like to think
my word wardrobe's as big
as my clothes vocabulary is small
and I suppose
one tiny faux pas, sartorial,
is no big deal
when you consider matters from this angle:

that someday all I might retrieve
when I'm groping for a simple cotton sleeve
or a soft off-rhyme for dingle-dangle
is a neurofibrillary hanger tangle.

Paula Tatarunis, MD

Pontine Ode

Oh, pons—what is more elegant
than your small name's simplicity?
Perhaps it's the complexity
beneath your corrugated front—

from yons and hithers fibers stream
across your bridge like refugees
from everywhere. Two aching knees,
a cadre of erotic dreams

from *mons veneris*, the left hand's
mislearned bass continuo
from a dull concerto grosso,
sleepily doodled ampersands.

as dons drone on into your eighth
cranial nerve, *pars cochlearis*,
and then you wish you were in Paris,
and that you hadn't lost your faith,

the *non*s and *oui*s of that debate
mingle with your inbreath, outbreath
then sluice down past life-or-death
from brain to hand. A poem? Great!

But cons approach, cadeucei poised
like bodkins at your prickling neck,
to pith you into doctors' heck
for smuggling in a poet's noise.

Mots bons are dripping off your tongue?
It's pinpoint pupils for you, Jack,
doll's-eyes staring midline, stuck,
their clockwork apparatus sprung.

ron rons all detached from doo doos,
while the voice of Neuroscience
ridicules your sad reliance
on medieval tropes and voodoos.

Eons from the cosmic clock
will lumber toward eternity
past postpostpostmodernity
and still the humble, white-clad doc,

peon of the ward and clinic,
will flog tired hearts with digitalis,
and sprinkle Freud on a limp phallus.
Pardon me. I am a cynic.

Neon poets, in the meantime,
strut and bray. Don't you adore them
slipping off *pons asinorum*?
(no rails or reason buttress rhyme.)

Oh pons, you are the swamped and slick
pontoon between disparities,
where we pratfall hilarities:
wrench the rhyme and scan the sick.

Paula Tatarunis, MD

Still Life

to J. G., dead of AIDS

Today, whether eating
yellow apples full of cool night,
or noticing the cool iridescence
of a black cat athwart a square
of yellow light, I think of you, dead,
of that which, like any thug, disarmed you first.

Desire unlocks the darkness of sweet fruit,
and wrests it from still life
like death will me from my red chair
and leave it behind, artifact of me,
for other eyes than mine to see
and also grieve my death.

And if black can iridesce, then death,
which seems so empty, must contain
everything: eye, chair, grief and all
the afternoon reveals and hides—
must contain like a great, dark backstage,
its actors resting up from the various

everlasting comedies of order and chaos.
Tragic with our taste
for the particular, comfortless
with desire, our flawed eyes
blurred with absence, we pray to see
our love return as light upon a leaf.

Paula Tatarunis, MD

Body Water

Yellow on green, those called up by the sun—
the daisy-likes and buttercups—deny
their origin from ashes, but the fringe
of moss and fern from which the first fall spills
warns softly, "What this flowing water wills
cannot be turned aside by anyone,
and no one can escape his origin."

The stream drops through volcano-spew to undermine
the hardened ash of rock, then overflows
to make a second fall from whence it goes
into the air as water dust and throws
back splintered prism colors sweet and cool
before it liquefies in jagged line
towards the third fall and its sandy pool.

Denying nothing, it began us all.
Water will rule, but even as it carves
the earth's burnt offering to grit and sand
it makes a garden as it polishes.
Basalt and pumice rear as palaces
penthoused with lilies and with pussy ears
to call a welcome to us as it lands
where salamanders hover, thrusting mouths
at caddis shadows falling from the air.

We come by river, in the water's care,
as water's shadows, leaving law and clock
to learn from fern and moss and polished rock.
We come from lands where water drains away
unnoticed though so much a part of us,
where time is short and no art long enough.

Here there is no human time or art.
The water rules. We step from buoyant rafts to fill
our eyes and fingertips with water's work,
and for the moment touch in body's ash
a source where flowing water works its will.

H. J. Van Peenen, MD

Starting the I.V.

I am good at this.
The arm bends out, the vein
lies stretched and succulent,
almost transparent under the sheen
of alcohol. My fingers slide
over the slippery skin, tracing
the engorgement.

He is frightened.
I see it in the tightness
of his muscles, so I tell him
I'm the best
and he eases, slightly.
The needle glides
under the skin, the beveled tip
lies alongside the vein
where I rest to let him
relax. It waits
like a mosquito attached
by its sucker,
lying in stillness
to disguise the pain.
I press the tip
against the bulbous column
and the wall bends, resisting
for an instant, then
as if capitulating, gives
and a column of blood
enters the tubing.
I am suddenly aware
I am connected to his brain.

I have learned not to hesitate here,
not to let fears of my own
about anesthesia, about loss
of control get in the way.
He will want to descend
quickly, not pausing
to feel each station of detachment.
I take the control he gives me
and bring him down.

H. David Watts, MD

MRI Scan

I arrive
in a place of strange
light, the kind
of place that takes away
intelligence.

I am dreamless.
I am made of the same stuff
the walls are made of.

I am a photograph.
The long door,
the closet, empty
in the center where I sit.

They say the magnet
draws particles
from air through the body,
energy that shakes the cells
and makes them cough up
their whereabouts.

I am a tube in a tube
with no exit sign,
a plastic cone
with sides that clack
and groan, my heart
shudders, my bones ache, I
could swear my skin rises
on a bed of crepitations
like tinfoil over Jiffy-Pop.

I can no longer tell
what is real. I imagine
the Van Allen Belt
sucked through my body,
my flesh shimmering like atmospheres
after space wind.

And I wonder
if now the soul
might leave the body
and drift as vapor

over the ordeal of tissues.
But then
the body would be alone.
So I lie still and witness
the dissection of my form.

And like Indians who feared
the photograph, knowing something
is lost there,
I wonder afterwards
if we ever are the same,
ever are,
after anything.

H. David Watts, MD

Soft Verge (near Coleshill)

He leans on air
between the hedge and road:
gray hair, gray jacket sagging from his shoulders
and those gray trousers too loose
to prop him up.
All day at the intersection, his wooden hands
dangle from the cuffs, his eyes stare
mask-empty at the traffic.
Motionless,
he slumps for hours,
some slack-jawed puppet hung up clumsily,
loose strings that we can't see
letting his head loll
not just toward his chest
but off slightly to one side.
Nothing moves him. Every day he waits
near the signpost to the village,
sun or rain on that same stretch of grass,
a stalled car of a man
that nothing can repair. He makes us pause
at the junction, keeps cautioning
like a semaphore stuck in one position
On our way to town each day,
he's a detour that we don't want to take.

Jane O. Wayne

Anaesthesia

How dark the water was,
when I dipped the oars
their pale hands disappeared.
I must have lost a year of nights
drifting on that lake.
while I slept, I might have been the cortex
in a tree, the bark around me
toughening, the wooden circles
widening their grasp.
I might have been enchanted in my bed,
might have let them steal my heart
and leave another.
What really happened?
Did I fall asleep under an elder tree
or is this the madness
of a strange heart pounding in my chest?
And in what forest of imagination
am I sleeping now?

Jane O. Wayne

Flowers After Surgery

Orchids, a calla lily
(they bloom again, mother),
sweetly tousled baskets (though two are identical,
like airplane salad).
Eleven sweetheart roses—
Loving gestures start to smother;
they make this invalid feel invalid.

(Silly, this need of another flower,
but where's the twelfth?
Filched? Or a sly florist's stealth?)
Drugs steal time in this hospital bower.

While I wander lonely as a cloud,
the last delivery crowds the sill:
a funereal bucket two feet high
spills delphinia, ranunculi
(obscenely tumorous homunculi)--
Pedunculated, the doctor said, but benign.
(A half-dozen, all mine.)
Did I mention the tuberous begonia?
Begone. Removed.

I am moved again
by friends, by knowledge that I didn't die—
At times, when on my couch I lie
in vacant or in pensive mood
I think of blooms and solitude
and know for sure with friends like these, who really
needs anemones?

Katharine Weber

The Song of Escherichia Coli

I live in your gut's glut, battening
on the sludgy tides, the sluiced excess
of crunch and guzzle, I float or sink
in churnings now gone slack, waved
onward sluggishly, or barnacle
the bottom, my populations clustering
on palp and polyp, their millionfold
silences crowding the darkness, their pale
anonymous history dogging yours.

Harbored in spoil and privacy, I make
manageable these embarrassments
of daily surplus, turning to myself
chaff, tailings, and dross, the fruit
of deglutition, nosing the wash
for bonus, in need of your prodigality
to keep me thronging and preserve
this hidden business, my occupation
and involvement, this partnership.

However havened, I lack impunity:
rumors disturb my teeming, echoes
of tumult and consternation tangle
and thwart the daily rhythms, the mix
smacks of fear or fury, or at times
I am beseiged by loosened freight
of indecipherable jettison, borne
as if from encounters of armadas
just beyond an occluding horizon.

Played out, hustled up, and expelled
as I am and shall be, yet I stay:
we have a journey to make together,
taking this strange confederacy
toward an ultimate banquet, where,
gathered now in the pooling and stillness,
I gluttonized outward toward daylight
on the very fabric of my world
in growing heedlessness and fury.

But not for me the rites of riddance—
thanks to your generosity, I came
to no conclusion, living on
to colonize your children's children,
distributed long ago on doorknob,
pencil, steering wheel, bedsheet,
handkerchief, drinking glass, even
(with luck) on goodnight kiss:
the seal and symbol of our union.

Charles B. Wheeler

Melissa's Last Cloud

Melissa floats—
She's on a cloud, in the cloud.
In the airplane now, she smiles;
the pilot sits her on his lap.
This time she really drives the plane.
Mother is anxious as she brings it in,
over the heads of startled people,
so soft a landing the passengers all clap.
Mother is always anxious. She should have known—

The cloud breaks. It's I.V. time again.
Melissa squinches up her face;
holds out her skinny, battered arm.
At least this time it isn't Johnson with the needle.
"Shaky Sam" the kids on the ward call him.
Today it's Carminita, who talks funny
but smiles a lot and finds the vein.

The clouds again—
She's in them almost all the time now.
Here she's pretty, and has hair
and no moon face, no ugly bruises.
She walks and runs
while floating on that cloud.

They thought she didn't hear them talking,
or wouldn't know their meaning,
"Resistant to all medications."
Even the littler kids on 'kemia ward
have figured that one out,
and know to hide away in clouds.

Melissa feels she's drifting far away.
Here's a bright and shining cloud.
It has a tunnel filled with light,
and voices of people she has known;
Gramps and Uncle John,
and children who had gone to I.C.U.
and—oh!—she sees them now.
Soundlessly she calls to them,
"Hello, it's me, Melissa."

Forrest P. White, MD

The Portugal Laurel

At times I fear,
after decades of doctoring,
of stashing tears in the pockets
of my long white coat,

my soul has turned to salt.

Take for example, the Portugal Laurel.
It has graced the patio for thirty-five years,
grown up with the family, seen sorrows, joys.
It has provided shade and beauty—
following a morning rain, it sparkles
in the afternoon sun, a million pieces
of dark green crystal, carnelian stems.
And, many a sleepless night, its branches
have hid the ashes of a slow cigar.
But now, children gone, the patio is a ruin.
The landscape architect proclaims,
"We need to open this space; it has to go."

So, yesterday I took the laurel down,
not the slightest hesitation. At the start,
I was occupied by technical matters—how to
bring down a robust laurel safely,
how to dispose of it. Never mind the details,
but, you know, I had to use a chain saw—
the trunk was twelve inches at the base.
In an hour and a half it was gone, all except
the weeping stump, an injured friend seeking
an explanation. Only then—only when
confronted by that personal void—
did I feel a single shiver of sadness.

See what I mean?

And today? Well, today
I have this pale blue numbness,
which I know by tomorrow
will be gone.

John L. Wright, MD

Therapy

—for Philip

You attribute my recovery
to nor trip tyline—
its effect on neuro-transmitters,
on the a myg dala.

You barely nod towards your worth—
insisting on blood levels,
on a therapeutic dose.

While I credit half our success
to the pear tree blossoming white
beyond your left shoulder,

to the wisteria—
its pink flowers hanging
lush and fragrant
over the portico,

to the warmth of your hand.

John L. Wright, MD

The Parade

for Nina, July 4, 1996

You cut out coupons, scan the "want ads."
You read the "lost and founds"
though you've not lost or found a thing.
You know the bag boy——a retired teacher,
works half time for health insurance,
the postal clerks——one just had his first
child, the other got caught with another man's wife.

You're part of everyman's story——the yardman's,
the teller's, the lawyer's, the window washer's,
the dentist's, the painter's, the pastor's.
You have long conversations on the phone,
laugh and weep over the line.
You converse daily with the dog and cat,
breakfast with friends every week.

You're the friendly thread in human webbing.

Like last week at the ball game:
in the fifth inning a stranger said,
after exchanging high fives,
"I feel like I've known you all my life."

Like yesterday: you dropped off the bottle
for a refill on my nortriptyline
and this morning you're telling me
the pharmacist doesn't like giving
large doses of antidepressants to the elderly,
he just filled a prescription for an old lady
he knows imbibes, his 36-year-old son
has been diagnosed with Parkinson's . . .

Like this afternoon: it's a sunny Fourth
and you're down on Main applauding the parade.
While here,
here in my green asylum above town,
I can barely hear
the people cheering,
the Drum and Bugle corps.

John L. Wright, MD

West on 172nd

for Jack Coulehan, physician and poet

I'm driving south on Meridian,
slowing for the light at 172nd.
A mixed-breed dog is approaching too,
trotting north,
trotting like it knows where it's going
—*like it's going home.*
I watch it jog towards me
through the intersection,
around east-bound cars,
slow down west-bound cars on the inside lane.
I grab my breath as it darts into the outside lane,
hear brakes squeal,
hear horns blow.
I hear the thud.
The lights change.
I drive east, head for I-5.
I'm going downtown to a ball game.

*Why didn't I get out of the car,
stop the traffic?*
I've asked that question before:
Why didn't I stop the insane plan
of flying Mrs. Mason to Tucson
for futile chemotherapy?
We sentenced her to a lonely death
1500 miles away.

No no, I don't miss a pitch.
But, between innings
I question my passivity, my fatalism:
have these twin
leaks drained all compassion
from my soul?
And I don't forget, either.
I'll forever see a yellow dog bounce six feet,
roll twice,
jump up and stagger west on 172nd
like a wino crossing 1st Avenue,
unaware of traffic,
headed ninety degrees
away from home.

John L. Wright, MD

A Lesser Chaos

In its zig-zagged scrawl
the cardiac monitor reminds me why I am
here on this see-through walled floor.
Lights from my machines punctuate the darkness
like stars. Gliding down the hallway
the nurses move as if made of foam
bobbing from room to room on midnight
rounds. Mine carries a flashlight,
its beam cutting through my room
like the blade of a sickle.
The monitor's blib blip bounces me alert
and I watch the signature of my heart trail off
into a long thin line.

Alarms, alarms.
A nurse wheels in
a crash cart, another
draws a syringe,
a third calibrates
my I.V. pumps. A doctor
cups my heel in his hand,
bangs his knuckles on my foot
to get a vein to rise.
Someone smears gel
on my torso and the overhead
light blares in its brilliant
white voice. I am dissolving
in its glare when two
surface pacemakers shock my chest,
the spasms through my breasts
wrest me from the mattress
again and again until the screen
attests to my heart's rhythmic gestures.

And then the procession files out—
the carts, poles and consoles,
the medical personnel.
Reflected in the glass
a lesser chaos—my pulse
tracing itself in green moonlight.

M. Wyrebek

Something From My Life

I am breathing deeply,
exhaling slowly,
I am relaxing my body,
toes, arches,
heels, ankles.
I imagine mermaids
swimming the warm waters
of my canals.
Their golden colors
swizzle through my body.
They hold aloft
in their hands—hands
as soft as earlobes—
White water lilies,
cupping them like votive candles.
These flowers are my cancer.
The mermaids deliver each cell
out of the cove of tumor.
Their glittery scales
lilt through my vessels.
My channels swell
with sun water
as mermaids stream
over lungs
down colon
past liver, spleen.

So many needles
jab my flesh.
So many tubes vent
through my neck,
chest, arms, groin.
Catheters snake like shadows
up my urinary tract,
down my nose,
along the femoral artery.
Scars pit and gouge my skin,
knick and serrate and mark
my whittled limbs like totem poles.
Someone may find my remains one day
and run his fingers over my brailled bones
to read something from my life
that he can take with him
on his way to wherever
he is going.

M. Wyrebek

The Student of Stones

for Alan Snyder

That day
they told him Molly's cancer
had come back

he went out into a field
and studied stones.
One stone

taught him how to sit
very still
in the sun, then how to release

all his warm dreams
into the purple night sky
like geese.

Another
taught him how to cup
each moment he had with her

about his body
like cool desert air
until it smelled like water.

And a third (for that day
they would put her
in the ground)

taught him how a stone
can crack seven ways
into dust.

George Young, MD